The Human Element in the Church of Christ

BY REV. PAUL SIMON
TRANSLATED FROM THE GERMAN BY
Meyrick Booth, Ph.D., (Jena)

the human element in the church of christ

WIPF & STOCK · Eugene, Oregon

Wipf and Stock Publishers
199 W 8th Ave, Suite 3
Eugene, OR 97401

The Human Element in the Church of Christ
By Simon, Paul and Booth, Meyrick
ISBN 13: 978-1-4982-9309-9
Publication date 3/22/2016
Previously published by The Newman Press, 1954

DEDICATED TO
KARL ADAM
FOR HIS
SIXTIETH BIRTHDAY

preface

THE following reflections upon the human element in the Church of Christ do not represent a theological treatise. They aim at presenting the human aspect of the life of the Church quite unsystematically, but in such fashion that the thinking man will understand the fundamentals of the question. No attempt has been made to deal with all the difficulties and objections that are encountered both inside and outside the Church. Many of the historical developments which might have been particularly helpful in an understanding of human influence in the Church have not been, of necessity, treated in this short study. Other subjects—such as the changes in the position of the clergy—have been lightly touched upon.

This book is dedicated to my dear friend Karl Adam, in grateful memory of our work together in Tübingen, and as a token of much that I owe to his stimulating personality.

PAUL SIMON

Paderborn, June 1, 1936.

contents

	Preface	vii
	Introduction to the 2016 Reprint Edition	xi
1.	The Temptations of Jesus	1
2.	The Humanity of Jesus	11
3.	The Human Element in the Early Church	18
4.	What Is Essentially Human in the Church?	29
5.	Perfection, Imperfection, and the Need for Reform	49
6.	Temptation Through Power	60
7.	Changes in the Position of the Clergy	72
8.	Criticism of the Church in Modern Times	91
9.	The Five Wounds of the Church	99
10.	Hindrances to the Spread of the Catholic Church in England	109
11.	Obstacles of the Early Twentieth Century	123
12.	The Occupational Dangers of the Clergy	133
13.	Organism and Organization	151
	Conclusion: *Civitas Dei*	163

Introduction to the 2016 Reprint Edition
The Threat of the Nazi Worldview and Catholic Apologetics

When the Nazi regime began to launch its most sinister attacks on the Catholic Church by charging hundreds of clergymen with financial fraud or immoral sexual actions, the former Tübingen professor Paul Simon (1882–1946)[1] published in 1936 this little book. It was no coincidence but strategic planning: Simon, who had taught apologetics and scholastic philosophy at one of Germany's most prestigious universities, Tübingen, realized that the attack on the moral integrity and reputation of the Church was more dangerous than either Alfred Rosenberg's *Myth of the Twentieth Century*, with its overt racism and hodgepodge of Nordic religions, or Jakob Wilhelm Hauer's idea of a Germanic Christianity "cleansed" of all "Jewishness." Until now, Catholics had stood by their Church and their pastors, but what if the Nazis should succeed in convincing a sizable minority of Catholics that most of their clergymen were embezzlers, or sexual predators, or practicing homosexuals?[2] Simon, however, decided not

---

1. Cf. Jörg Ernesti, "Paul Simon (1882–1946)—Humanist und Pionier der Ökumene," *Catholica* 58 (2004) 296–313.

2. Josef Höfer, "Erinnerungen an Dompropst Professor Dr. Paul Simon," in Paul-Werner Scheele (ed.), *Paderbornensis Ecclesia* (Paderborn: Schöningh,

to address the mostly invented charges, but rather the more fundamental theological problem lurking underneath: how can one trust and believe in a Church full of sinners, especially if they are entrusted with leadership positions and are members of the hierarchy?

Catholics read the book eagerly, and within a few months Herder Verlag in Freiburg issued a second edition. Yet the success of the little volume was such a thorn in the side of the regime that this second edition was banned. The German secret police had labeled it a "harmful" book—which is remarkable since it does not mention National Socialism or Hitler. Nonetheless, it fulfilled its purpose, namely, to inoculate German Catholics against Nazi propaganda. Moreover, it offered them an intellectually convincing explanation of why one could still trust the Church but could not realistically expect her to be a community of saints alone.

In fact, a large number of forbidden theological and philosophical works were not directly criticizing the Nazis but instead offering a persuasive account of an alternative worldview, thereby rivaling Nazi doctrine. This makes it necessary for the historian to investigate the context of published material even more carefully: if the Nazis perceived such works as threats to their agenda despite the already extremely narrow boundaries in which Catholic publishing could continue to exist, then we have to take them more seriously than has hitherto been done. In fact, research on the works of censored theologians and Christian philosophers has usually overlooked those works that do not explicitly deal with a defense of the Jews, politics, or the war. To a certain extent, the reason seems to be that these texts require the reader to have a theological or philosophical background to understand their subtle, implicit attacks on Nazi thought. Another reason in my view, however, is the prejudice that the theologico-philosophical task of battling the Nazi worldview in order to inoculate against its ideas was a negligible endeavor. Many historians are so fixated on what the churches have said "explicitly" on this or that topic that many overlook what has

---

1972) 631–88.

Introduction to the 2016 Reprint Edition xiii

been said *between the lines*. This does not mean that we should think of the churches as uniform bulwarks against Nazism or whitewash their records, but merely that the focus on certain research objectives has eclipsed others. If one reads the Catholic literature of the period between 1933 and 1945, one finds numerous allusions to and implicit criticisms of the regime, which one could call "immanent" apologetics—the attempt to make the faith more intelligible and more defensible against Nazi criticism.

The authors who belong in this category are legion but often go unnamed in history books. I would like to mention just three examples of outspoken direct and indirect apologetics from the archdiocese of Paderborn, to which Simon belonged: the Franciscan Desiderius Breitenstein publicly criticized Houston Stewart Chamberlain and the Nazi ideology of blood and race in a number of brochures and articles, one of which was forbidden; Bernhard Lakebrink destroyed the Nazi claim that the medieval mystic Meister Eckhart was one of theirs; and Hans Pfeil published there two censored works in which he disclosed the logical inconsistencies and fallacies of Nazi theology. Again, these are examples from just one town, and thus only the tip of the iceberg![3] This does not mean that every theologian in Paderborn worked against the regime; most famously, Josef Mayer (1886–1967) embraced Nazi eugenics.[4] Rather, we have to become better aware of the subtle theologico-philosophical discussions and agendas if we want to arrive at an adequate description and analysis of Catholicism and other Christian churches during the Third Reich (1933–45). This

---

3. Desiderius Breitenstein, *Begegnung von Kirche und Welt* (Hildesheim: Borgmeyer, 1936); Breitenstein, *Geist oder Blut?* (Paderborn: Bonifacius, 1934); Bernhard Lakebrink [anonymously], "Meister Eckhart," in *Studien zum Mythos des 20. Jahrhunderts* (Cologne: Bachem, 1934); Hans Pfeil, *Der deutsche Glaube in philosophischer Sicht* (Paderborn: Bonifacius, 1935); Pfeil, *Der Mensch im Denken der Zeit* (Paderborn: Schöningh, 1937).

4. Kathrin Brüggenthies, "Die Philosophisch-Theologische Akademie Paderborn," in Dominik Burkard and Wolfgang Weiss (eds.), *Katholische Theologie im Nationalsozialismus* (Würzburg: Echter, 2011) 1:208–50.

spiritual resistance of Catholics has not been on the horizon of historians. In fact, most have never read Simon's book even though it is programmatic of how Catholics thought they could work to avert the worst: by using the remaining narrow means of publicizing religious texts and thereby defending the teachings of the Church on faith and morality (including natural law).[5] Again, I am not suggesting that the Church was universally heroic (it was especially among the hierarchy quite timid) but simply that there is more to the story than we usually acknowledge.

Paul Simon was not unknown in prewar Catholicism. He had since his youth been a close friend of the last democratic chancellor of Germany, the Catholic politician Heinrich Brüning (1885–1970).[6] Simon was involved in a renewal of scholastic thought that is widely forgotten or ignored today. Instead of following a narrow theology, Simon dialogued with modern philosophy, in particular phenomenology, and honestly admitted where the shortcomings of Aquinas lay.[7] He took a stance against strict neo-Thomists and argued that the proofs for the existence of God should be freely discussed, because the First Vatican Council had never declared that an irrefutable proof of God's existence had been found and established. Instead, Simon described the proofs along the lines of theology as a whole: as the never-ending search for making faith intelligible, as a perennial quest for evidence. "The proofs for the existence of God have to be on the table for discussion," he wrote. "After all, only the natural ability of

---

5. Cf. Raimund Baumgärtner, *Weltanschauungskampf im Dritten Reich: Die Auseinandersetzung der Kirchen mit Alfred Rosenberg* (Mainz: M. Grünewald, 1977); cf. Dominik Burkard, "Gebundene Hände? Oder: Wie dem Nationalsozialismus begegnen?," *Theologie und Glaube* 104 (2014) 3–31.

6. Jörg Ernesti, *Ökumene im Dritten Reich* (Paderborn: Bonifacius, 2007) 329.

7. The most important book of this movement was probably Hans Meyer, *Thomas von Aquin* (Bonn: P. Hanstein, 1938; 2nd ed., 1961); translated by Frederic Eckhoff as *The Philosophy of St. Thomas Aquinas* (St. Louis: Herder, 1944).

Introduction to the 2016 Reprint Edition

the human intellect to recognize the existence of God through the contemplation of creation was defined a dogma."[8]

Such openness to a critical examination of the tradition should not surprise us—after all he was a student of Albert Erhard (1862–1940) and Clemens Baeumker (1853–1924), who were among the pioneers of a critical history of theology, and thus showed that one could not merely import Aquinas into modernity without realizing his historical limitations (as Kleutgen did). First teaching at the academy in Paderborn, in 1925 Simon was appointed professor of scholastic philosophy and apologetics at the University of Tübingen, where he became a colleague of Karl Adam (1876–1966), arguably the most prominent Catholic theologian of his time but unfortunately blind to the dangers of Nazism. Like Albert Lang (1890–1973) in Bonn, Simon viewed apologetics not as a polemic and controversialist exercise but rather as an immanent enterprise: the intelligibility of the faith should be demonstrated and dialogue with the churches of the Reformation sought: "The positive exposition and vivid reality of the Catholic life of faith ... has more effect than all the polemic in the world."[9] Already in the year of his appointment to Tübingen he published a widely acclaimed little book on the reunification of the churches. To the astonishment of many of his colleagues, Simon declared that due to the fragmentation of Christianity, even the Catholic Church could no longer realize the fullness of what Jesus had desired when he founded the Church. The churches, he insisted, had to come together to battle the spread of atheism. Soon he was regarded as the leading Catholic in German ecumenical circles. Ecumenism, however, was considered a potential threat to the Nazi regime, because it could weld the churches together.[10]

---

8. Paul Simon, "Die natürliche Gotteserkenntnis und die Entscheidung des Vatikanischen Konzils," *Philosophisches Jahrbuch* 53 (1940) 78–96.

9. Quoted in Höfer, "Erinnerungen," 647.

10. Cf. Jörg Ernesti, *Ökumene im Dritten Reich*; Ernesti, "Paderborn und die Ökumene im Dritten Reich: Annäherungen der Kirchen unter dem Druck des Regimes," *Theologie und Glaube* 104 (2014) 82–104.

Simon was so universally liked by all confessions that he was elected rector of the University of Tübingen. In 1933 he resigned, probably due to pressure from the minister of culture, and returned to Paderborn to take up the position of dean of the Cathedral. Yet Simon still published. The fact that his writings avoided polemic and instead relied on emotionless argumentation made them the best apologetic tool in the fight against the regime. Consequently, the Nazi censors also banned his books *Worldview* (1935) and *Myth or Religion* (2nd ed., 1936), which refuted the racist and materialist program of the Nazi Party's chief ideologue, Alfred Rosenberg (1893–1946). Nevertheless, Simon saw no legitimization for the Church to support direct resistance beyond such intellectual battles and Pope Pius XI's encyclical *Mit brennender Sorge* (1937).[11] He died unexpectedly in 1946, in Paderborn.

Along with *The Human Element in the Church of Christ*, Simon's many other writings deserve to be reread, not just by theologians and historians but by all the faithful. Unlike others who tried to build bridges to Nazism by appealing to Catholicism as "culture," Simon remained unwavering in preaching that the Church's mission was to proclaim *Christ*. In 2016, his words from 1936 could have been uttered with the same force by Pope Francis: "The Church did not come to disseminate culture in the Western sense of the word, but to save souls."[12]

—Ulrich L. Lehner

---

11. Ernesti, "Paul Simon," 303.

12. Simon, *Das Menschliche in der Kirche Christi*, 2nd ed. (Freiburg: Herder, 1936) 62.

The Human Element in the Church of Christ

chapter 1 · The Temptations of Jesus

THE Gospel of St. Matthew tells us that, immediately after being baptized by John the Baptist, Jesus was led by the Spirit into the wilderness to be tempted by the devil: "And after fasting forty days and forty nights, he was hungry. And the tempter came and said to him . . ." (Matt. 4:2-3).* Thus we see that the temptations came to Jesus when He had completed the preparation for His public life. If these temptations are placed so prominently at the beginning of Jesus' period of active work in the world, they must be regarded as of special significance. They are not the temptations which might be set before a private individual. The decisions required to meet them do not concern an individual: they concern the Saviour and His *calling*. This compels us to assume that the temptations were such as to turn Him away from the true nature of His calling, that they were directed against the essence of His mission on earth. Thus we can perceive in these temptations the *typical dangers* to the mission of Christ and to Christianity itself. The Gospels describe them as the temptations of the Messiah Himself; but they are, at the same time, dangers besetting the Apostles and the Church.

Three temptations are described in the Gospel; and we shall deal with them in the order found in St. Matthew. The first

---

* All quotations from the New Testament are taken from the Confraternity of Christian Doctrine edition of the New Testament, St. Anthony Guild Press, Paterson, New Jersey, 1947.

was concerned with the need of the man Jesus for food: "If thou art the Son of God, command that these stones become loaves of bread." The natural consequence of the prolonged fast was hunger. The need of the body for food and drink is a matter-of-course for every human being. This *human* fact of hunger is in no way denied or concealed by the Gospel. There is the straightforward statement: "he was hungry." The natural reaction would have been to look for food and drink. This was the point of attack for the tempter. He suggests the *creation* of food and drink: "If thou art the Son of God"! This is the preliminary condition, the obvious train of thought is—*then* you will have the power to help yourself in such a small difficulty as this! The tempter makes no offer to help. He merely suggests that Jesus should make use of the power given to Him.

Hunger is the type of the bodily or, more generally, the earthly needs. The question is: will He make use, or can He properly make use, of the power attached to His mission for the satisfaction of His bodily and earthly needs? In order fully to understand the meaning of the Evangelist we must weigh properly the answer given by Jesus. He did *not* say that it was unworthy for the Messiah to care about food and drink. He did not even directly refuse the suggestion, but pointed out that the life of man has a far wider significance than is found in mere bodily existence. And because it is greater than the physical, the spiritual takes the first place; our life is dependent upon the Word of God and the nourishment thus derived is more important than earthly food. The refusal to be tempted does not, therefore, depend upon the office of Messiah. Rather does the Messiah tell the tempter that he fails to recognize the true nature of human life, and overvalues the power of earthly needs in the case of those who know their own real calling. When we become conscious of our real being, we know that

The Temptations of Jesus

every sort of bodily and earthly need must be borne for the sake of a higher purpose and indeed *can* be borne, when our spiritual needs are fully satisfied. The concept of earthly need can be extended to include all that is needful for earthly existence—the whole of our natural life with its aims, wishes and needs. What we understand by culture and civilization is included in this category. In the really *decisive* hour, it must give way to the call of God. Jesus did not say that it is unworthy to satisfy hunger and thirst, or that it is unseemly for the Messiah to suffer hunger and thirst. He made it clear that the higher spiritual life must so predominate that earthly needs take second place. Looking at this temptation from a general viewpoint, it signifies that one departs from the true meaning of the religious calling, if earthly aims are pursued by means of the power attaching to a *religious* mission. This does not mean that earthly aims should not be pursued at all, that they are sinful or that they should not be recognized by the servants of God, but only that these should not place their mission at the service of earthly aims. Religion must never be a *means*. It is an end in itself—and the highest end!

Applying this lesson to the Church, its significance is that its position in the world and its mission to humanity carries with it the inevitable danger that the individual, by reason of his privileged position, by virtue of his activity on behalf of the Christian mission, may seek to secure special worldly advantages. It is not asked of him that he should suffer hunger or thirst—merely that his hunger and thirst, and other worldly needs, should not be satisfied by a misuse of religious powers! In the same way, the Church, as a community, must not subordinate the mission entrusted to it to earthly aims. It was not founded by Christ to satisfy cultural needs, but to preach the Gospel and to save souls. The cultural forms and institutions which the Church uses in the furtherance of its mission must never assume the character of ends in themselves. They must remain means to the higher end.

The second temptation is equally characteristic: "Then the devil took him into the holy city and set him on the pinnacle of the temple, and said to him, 'If thou art the Son of God, throw thyself down; for it is written, "He will give his angels charge concerning thee; and upon their hands they shall bear thee up, lest thou dash thy foot against a stone"'" (Matt. 4:5–6).

It makes no difference whether we regard this temptation as a vision, or as an actual raising up to a height upon the temple. The tempter does not, of course, suggest to the Messiah that He should claim only the fulfilment of the promise of the Old Testament; this temptation strikes at the very heart of His office. By a pinnacle is clearly intended a height visible from the courts of the temple, which were filled with people on days of festival, so that the Messiah, when He sprang or (better still) was borne through the air by angels, would be seen, of necessity, by large numbers of people. That is the point: an outstanding sign or miracle should be given before the people; for the Jews demanded such a sign. (See Matt. 12:38; 16:1; Mark 8:11.) Thus the suggestion of the tempter was that Jesus should, at the very beginning of His Messianic calling, exploit the crude desire of the multitude for a miracle, and show the crowd that the promises of Psalm 91 applied to Him, thus supplying a convincing proof that He was the Messiah. The people would then have been won over by a single stroke, and the Messianic "revolution" could have begun. All the spectators would have known that here, indeed, was the Son of God, visibly protected by His Father. All the suffering, trouble, preaching and disappointment, with the hard struggle to win the soul of the people would have been superfluous. Once and for all, He would have been recognized as Messiah.

Again, Jesus answered with a saying from the Scriptures, not, however, with reference to the impossibility of awakening belief by a species of jugglery, but by describing the deed suggested by the tempter as a temptation of God: "Thou shalt not tempt the Lord thy God." It was wrong to appeal wantonly to God in a situation when the help of God could not legitimately be reckoned upon. Again we note that He did not reject miracles *as such*, even if they caused popular astonishment. In the Gospel we find numerous examples of acts which aroused the astonishment of the multitude. More than once we are told that many believed because they had witnessed a sign. St. John even tells us that the crowd wanted to take Him away to make Him king (John 6:15) after the miracle of the loaves and fishes. On the other hand, Jesus energetically repudiated the demand of the Jews that He work a miracle. The form of miracle suggested by the tempter, therefore, possessed a special character of its own, and one that made its rejection essential: it was wholly inappropriate to the proclamation of the Gospel. For what the devil suggested was that the crowd should be so impressed by a sensational miracle that they would follow the Messiah under the influence of mass-psychology, and *not* through genuine inner conviction. Furthermore, the Saviour cannot allow His acts to be prescribed. He was, from time to time, amenable to human requests; but these were granted only when such action did not run contrary to His mission. In a word, the Messiah repudiated all means that did not correspond with the mission of spreading the Kingdom of God. And this cannot come, like a political movement, through a wave of popular enthusiasm sweeping the masses along; it can come only through taking hold of men's hearts and innermost selves. The Kingdom does not demand an outward enthusiasm—soon so likely to pass away—but a deep inward conviction, with renewal of life and repentance. For this reason St. Matthew quotes the text from Isaiah: " 'Behold, my servant, whom I have chosen, my beloved in whom my soul is well pleased: I will put my Spirit upon him, and he will declare judgment to the Gentiles. He will not wrangle, nor cry aloud, neither will anyone hear his voice in the streets. A bruised reed he will not break, and a smoking wick he will not quench, till he send forth judgment unto victory' " (Matt. 12:18–20).

It is, therefore, clear that the second temptation signifies, in its application to the Church, that such means as we have described cannot be employed in the service of the Faith: namely, such as appeal to credulity and mass-instinct, and not to man's conscience and sense of responsibility. It is not desired that human means of influencing the masses, if acceptable in character, should be neglected. Religious services, together with their accompanying ceremonies, exert a psychological influence upon the masses; so did the miracles performed by Jesus Himself. A rebirth of the spirit can, at times, result in this manner. But such means must be rejected without hesitation, if their aim should be to overwhelm men in the absence of a genuine inward conviction.

In the third temptation Jesus is led to the summit of a high mountain and sees the kingdoms of this world and their glory spread out before Him. The tempter says: "All these things will I give thee, if thou wilt fall down and worship me." The devil here appears as the ruler of the whole world, with all its glory. The kingdoms of this world are indicted in an *empirical sense*, and the glory includes all that comes under the head of worldly power, honor, and glory. He presents himself as the lord of all these things and in a position to place them in the hands of the Messiah, given His acceptance of the overlordship of the ruler of this world.

This temptation provides the sharpest contrast to the ideal of the Messiah. Its chief point lies in the fact that a section of the Jews awaited a political Messiah. The question whether Jesus will or will not satisfy the political claims of the Jews is forced thereby into the open. Political power and worldly authority, as expected by the Jews, is completely opposed to the authority of the Gospel. The former seeks material power and outward success, seeing therein its highest standard of values; and, though not devoid of ideas, these are such that they cannot be realized save through material power. To the Saviour is offered political and material power, after the fashion of this world, if He will bow down before the principle of power and success and admit its validity in the religious field.

Jesus finally and completely rejects the offer of the tempter, again quoting the Scriptures: "Begone, Satan! for it is written, 'The Lord thy God shalt thou worship and him only shalt thou serve.'" He thus passes judgment upon the path suggested by the tempter: the path indicated by the Jewish ideal. It runs contrary to the will of God for, considered fundamentally, it dethrones God, setting up the world in His place. To place too high a value upon worldly success in the religious field is displeasing to God: it constitutes an attack upon truth and upon the true hierarchy of values. Power and success can be given to the evil forces, to antichrist—nay, in this world of original sin, they may be given *more* readily to these than to the chosen of God! All the more reason why the Messiah should so sharply reject such methods.

What is the application of this temptation for the Church? Political domination must never be regarded as a *goal* for the activities of the Church, and means which might be acceptable in the political field must not be employed in religious work. The Church will always encounter political powers in the course of its history. These powers will certainly seek either to place themselves at the service of the Church, or to make use of it for their own purposes. Either of these possibilities may occur without losing sight of the one true aim: the worship of God. But it must be admitted that here temptation threatens; and it must be firmly rejected if the Church is to perform its true task.

The temptations, as described by Matthew, indicate a progressive increase in severity. It would seem that the last is the greatest and most dangerous. The first is the most easily understood, speaking humanly, and thus, despite its danger, is not so serious a departure from the true path as are the other two. The servants of the Church, the bearers of its power, are no more than *human* and always open to temptation. Their wishes, interests and needs remain human. Thus, situations can continually arise in which the weak human element misuses religion.

The typical temptations capable of attacking the essence of the Christian mission itself are given to us in the Gospels. They occur again and again in the course of Church history. And whenever men, being representatives of the Church, succumb to them we find corruption and decay within the Church. These are the temptations described in the divine revelation itself as the special dangers threatening the Kingdom of God. Should the Church succumb to them it would have forgotten its essential task and reversed the true direction of its mission. The temptations overcome by Christ were not overcome once and for all for individual holders of ecclesiastical power. On the contrary, we understand from the Gospels that they will continue to assail those called to leadership of the Church, otherwise they would not be the typical temptations of the Kingdom. It is quite possible that individual dignitaries of the Church, or even whole periods of history, may succumb more or less; but it is impossible that the Church as a whole and *as such* should fail to resist the dangers, since it would then no longer be the Church of Christ!

The three temptations of Jesus are set forth as the special dangers besetting the Messiah and the Church itself. They are thus the obstacles encountered by Jesus Himself: the causes of offense rejected by God. This does not signify that the opponents of the Church (or lukewarm members thereof) will take offense should the representatives of the Church fail in their resistance to them. The Jews, to whom Christ brought the Gospel, took offense upon quite other issues.

The second temptation was often repeated by the Pharisees when they desired a sign: "Master, we would see a sign from thee" (Matt. 12:38; 16:1). In rejecting the request, Jesus said: "An evil and adulterous generation demands a sign, and no sign shall be given it but the sign of Jonas the prophet." The Pharisees did not say, at least according to the Gospel account, that they made their belief dependent upon a sign; but this request can hardly have had any other meaning, since such a sign was clearly a means of establishing the legitimacy of Jesus' mission. Did they not ask on various occasions by whose authority He acted? (Matt. 21:23). To His severe judgment upon the generation that rejected Him, Jesus added: "The men of Nineve will rise up in the judgment with this generation and will condemn it; for they repented at the preaching of Jonas, and behold, a greater than Jonas is here. The queen of the South will rise up in the judgment with this generation and will condemn it; for she came from the ends of the earth to hear the wisdom of Solomon, and behold, a greater than Solomon is here" (Matt. 12:41–42). A connection is seen between the attitude of the Pharisees and the second temptation. They are not inwardly ready to accept the call to repentance uttered by Jesus: "Repent, for the kingdom of heaven is at hand." Their souls do not yearn for the true wisdom coming from God, but they would like Jesus to perform a juggler's act for their benefit: an act that would *compel* their belief, although the true inward contacts, needful for belief were totally lacking. They are hardened; their minds are closed against wisdom; they sin against the Holy Ghost: "Every kind of sin and blasphemy shall be forgiven to men; but the blasphemy against the Spirit will not be forgiven" (Matt. 12:31).

The third temptation is also thrown into relief by the attitude of the Jews and especially of the Pharisees. Their expectations are directed towards a political Messiah. They take offense at the fact that Jesus did not come to establish a new worldly kingdom, but a kingdom of the spirit.

We thus have two categories of offenses: the true offense that is also an offense in the eyes of God, deriving from the violation of the true order; and the false offense deriving from the rejection of the false ideas and desires of non-believers and those lukewarm in the Faith.

chapter 2 · The Humanity of Jesus

It is not the purpose of this chapter to explain the dogmatic teaching as to the true humanity of Jesus. We are concerned solely to show that the humanity of Jesus in the revelation of the New Testament is of extraordinary importance in the history of salvation, not only for the period spent by Jesus upon this earth but also for the form taken by His Church. It is one of the dogmas of the Church that Jesus was really and truly a man. All attempts to obscure this fact have, throughout the centuries, been sharply rejected by the Church. He was not only in *appearance* a man; He was not a species of ghost or insubstantial being, bearing the likeness of man as a covering or disguise: He was a *genuine man*, in body and soul. The New Testament itself leaves no doubt upon this matter. It gives us a picture of the man Jesus, from His birth until His death. Even if the picture presented to us in the Gospels is intended with special reference to the revelation, at least it is certain that the Christ and Messiah revealed in this picture in the Gospels is the same preached of by Paul as the glorified, who lived and died, as a man, in Palestine at a definite time.

It must be admitted that the Gospels do not give us, anywhere, a description of His outward appearance which would allow us to form a definite picture of Him as man. In fact, this is so pointedly avoided that we are driven to assume that there was nothing outstanding about His outward appearance such as would mark Him out as different from those around Him. None of the Evangelists say anything about His physical character or about His beauty, although, in many other ways, they give a clear picture of Him as a man. In the case of His birth, the poverty-stricken nature of His environment provided a startling contrast to the importance of His entry into this world. The glory of Heaven must have lit up, at least for a moment, that all too poor setting. Of His boyhood days we know only of the one event in Jerusalem that showed Him for a short time in a particular situation; the Gospels tell us that men were astounded by His wisdom. The desire of apocryphal writers to furnish the youth of Jesus with all kinds of extraordinary miracles is specially significant, since it emphasizes the extreme sobriety of the Gospel narrative, which tells us plainly that He grew up in the seclusion of a carpenter's house. That He went about in Palestine preaching would hardly have been anything out of the way at that time. In any case, the narrative tells us that He took part in all human affairs. He was entertained by His friends, ate and drank with them, and participated in all their joys and sorrows. He had not only disciples but real *friends,* and the Jews noted that He wept at the grave of His friend Lazarus. Jesus Himself told us that He did not—like John—lead an ascetic life, and that public opinion sometimes made this a cause of offense; and He employed a very drastic expression to characterize the talk of the crowd: ". . . [men call me a] glutton and a wine-drinker" (Matt. 11:19). The fatigue of the journey and the heat make Him tired and He rests in some shady place and asks for food and drink. Now and then He is overcome by fatigue and He sleeps like a man so over-tired that He no longer notices the dangers about Him. His humanity becomes very clear when His sufferings begin. He foresees the betrayal

The Humanity of Jesus

by one of his disciples, and gives a reserved but clear expression to His sorrow. Foreseeing His dreadful death, He is so overcome with spiritual distress that a sweat of agony breaks out upon His forehead—a truly *human* picture! He knows that He must suffer and He takes this willingly upon Him, but He seeks to take it in a human way, not, like the self-centered stoics, with a display of false heroics. Even upon the Cross He gives expression to His dreadful agony in the cry: "My God, my God, why hast thou forsaken me?" His conduct before the tribunal was that of a true man. He did not recognize the competence of Herod, and did not deign to give him a reply. When brought before Pilate, He remained silent; and He knew how to deal with unjust treatment by a firm, quiet, dignified refusal to accept it. The same Man who on another occasion said: "if some one strike thee on the right cheek, turn to him the other also" (Matt. 5:39), protested energetically, but with dignity, against the improper conduct of an overzealous servant of the high priest (John 18:23).

Beyond all doubt, we see in all this that Christ wished to go about among men as a true man, that He wanted in all respects —apart from sin—to be as other men. This humanity was a cause of offense to the Jews. The narrow nationalistic standpoint of the Jews had caused them to form a picture of a *political* savior in whom all their political desires had taken shape. The Messiah must be a great hero raised far above all that was human: a great political figure able to seize power, destroy the Roman Empire and place the Jews in a position of world-dominance. But the Christ of the Gospels rejected all such claims. He appeared in poverty, clothed with human weakness; and, to the Jews—who saw in their savior no more than a means of satisfying their national egoism—He was a stumbling block. He remained calmly and confidently aloof from political ambitions and decisions. He was neither prepared to follow the easily excited masses and allow Himself to be crowned king (John 6:15), nor to give decisive instructions as to how the people were to behave towards the Romans. His answer to the question of the Pharisees, as to whether one should pay taxes to the emperor, was in reality a refusal of the question. His answer exposed the hypocrisy of the Jews, for, by indicating the coin in common use among them, He made it clear that they had long compromised with the Roman overlordship, and that they did not refuse to do business with the Romans and grow rich thereby. The payment of taxes thus became a matter of no further importance.

The imagination of the people had created a specific picture of the Messiah. They expected him in human form, since he was to rule over the Jews and, as the representative of the Jewish kingdom, over the whole world; but they envisaged him as a human hero, by taking away from him every human weakness. This may sound paradoxical, but it corresponds with mass psychology. The crowd seeks always to make a mythical figure of its hero, according to which he incorporates a wish-fulfilment, being endowed with superhuman powers and free from real human nature with its weaknesses. This process does not aim at the removal from the hero of all human characteristics; certain human qualities are presumed present in the hero of the masses. But these qualities must not contradict the egoism of the crowd nor, in many cases, its lower instincts. In the case of the Jewish Messiah, it was expected of him in the very first place that he should be clothed with power and glory, and be an instrument of popular revenge against the Romans.

The cult of this idea in the people caused the picture to become developed and altered in the course of time. The result was a firmly established political myth. It was this, in particular, that Jesus energetically rejected and contradicted

The Humanity of Jesus

with every fiber of His human nature, with all His words and deeds. He had no desire for political power and no wish to approach men from the political angle. The fact of His humanity was a living contradiction of the whole picture of the Messiah, as seen by the Jews: in short, He was the stumbling block. On the one hand, they saw His sharp rejection of the political ideal and of political means for establishing the kingdom of God; on the other, they were offended by His human nature, with its weakness, which He had not disdained to take upon Him, despite His calling. It was not the Pharisees alone who felt thus. His own fellow-countrymen in Nazareth could not accept Him, knowing, as they did, so much about His humble origin. Did they not all know that He was the son of the carpenter Joseph; and did they not know all His relations? It was obvious that *this* man could not be called to a high mission.

Jesus as a human being is the pattern of the Church. He became a true man in order to save men, and founded His Church as a Church of men for men. Never did He think of the Church as free from human weakness. The state of complete perfection and final glory was not placed by Him at the beginning of the historic mission, but at the end. If the Church is His body, then there must be manifested in the visible body of the Church all the weaknesses which He bore upon earth, and this human frailty must remain as an inevitable cause of offense all down the ages. Jesus was sinless: but, in the case of the men who make up the body of the Church on earth, no human weakness—including sin—can be excluded. All human temptations that can lead men astray are possible temptations for members of the Church—not only for a portion of the Church or for a special class of people, but for *all* Christians. However great may be the services of a man for the Kingdom of God, there can be no guarantee that he is free from human weakness.

This 'humanity' possesses a special importance in the history of the Church and of human salvation. The Church, as the body of Christ throughout the ages, puts forward the same claims as those advanced by Christ Himself in His own age. He demanded belief from men; so does the Church. It certainly cannot be denied that, in the course of time, the Church has become an imposing organization—even in a worldly sense. More especially among non-Catholics, the greatness of the world embracing Church is constantly emphasized: the organization, the methods employed in the care of souls, the deep understanding of the soul of the people, all these are the subject of frequent praise. Many reject the idea of the Church as a supernatural institution founded by Christ, yet they cherish a sincere admiration for it. Others take the view that the Church is a cunningly contrived invention of the human mind, or of a particular class or group of people. Both schools of thought—those who admire and those who reject—are at one in making of the Church a purely human and natural institution; above all, they are united in presenting to the eyes of the faithful a picture of the Church as so imposing, so fascinating, so super-subtle, that the supernatural mission of the Church is thrust out of sight and belief becomes superfluous.

But it is stated in the Scriptures that God has chosen the weak and lowly * and Jesus speaks not only to His Apostles, but to the Church, in calling them the "little flock." Thus, for the faithful, the human side of the Church becomes a touchstone of belief. Those who admire the Church from outside would like to tread the path suggested in the second tempta-

---
* See 1 Cor. 1:27 and Matt. 11:25.

tion of Christ: the Church is to be an instrument so cleverly thought out and so beautifully organized that faith would no longer be a grace and free decision, but a natural product formed by earthly means. The humanity of Jesus is beyond doubt a deep mystery. The natural man may well ask why Jesus chose to appear in such lowly fashion; why He did not make use of all the unlimited means at His disposal for convincing the people. The same question may be put in respect to the Church: why must its members be twisted in their minds and led astray by misunderstanding, inadequacy, sin and disgrace? But if this were not the case, the Church would no longer be an object of *faith* and the continuation of Christ, who suffers all things and is yet victorious; it would be no more than a political instrument, adapted to this world, producing earthly convictions by earthly means.

chapter 3 · The Human Element in the Early Church

CARDINAL NEWMAN stated in a sermon that St. Paul had good reason to feel a special pride in being able to apply to himself the ancient saying: *homo sum, humani nihil a me alienum puto*—I am a man and nothing human is alien to me. The genuine humanity of Paul is never concealed in his letters; on the contrary, it is prominently displayed. He admits freely to a knowledge of his faults and weaknesses. It can be understood that his record as a one-time persecutor of Christians, converted by a wonderful experience of grace into an Apostle of Christ, would not lower him in the eyes of his converts and followers. But he knew also that it was being said of him in the Christian communities that he had enemies who saw his faults more clearly than did his friends, opponents who declared, cynically, that his letters were indeed powerful but that his bodily presence was weak and his speech contemptible (2 Cor. 10:10). We do not know what he really looked like; but it would seem that there was nothing impressive about him. He tells us himself of the illness that tormented him. This was sent, he says, by God, that he should not fall a victim to pride and be exalted above measure: "There was given me . . . a messenger of Satan, to buffet me" (2 Cor. 12:7). He admits that his power is made perfect in infirmity (2 Cor. 10:9), and finds glory in his infirmities. His frankness in speaking of all these things gives a peculiarly *personal* note to his work, and an individual position among the missionaries. His temperament shines through his letters. Continually he speaks of his sorrows and joys. Nothing is kept back. His life was one of sacrifice and struggle, together with all the physical hardships associated at that time with travel, especially for those not possessed of means.

Very openly he speaks of his work: "in many more labors, in prisons more frequently, in lashes above measure, often exposed to death. From the Jews five times I received forty lashes less one. . . . In labor and hardships, in many sleepless nights, in hunger and thirst, in fastings often, in cold and nakedness" (2 Cor. 11:23, 24, 27). All this is put before us in the simplest manner and without egoism. He was justified in stating that all the sorrows of the Christian communities were borne also by him: "Besides those outer things, there is my daily pressing anxiety, the care of all the churches! Who is weak, and I am not weak? Who is made to stumble and I am not inflamed?" (2 Cor. 11:28). St. Paul never exhibits the stereotyped features of a conventional saint's picture. As a Christian and an Apostle of the Lord, he is still well able to scold and denounce. He rages against the Galatians: "O foolish Galatians! who has bewitched you. . . ." (Gal. 3:1), and again: "But though we or an angel from heaven should preach a gospel to you other than that which we have preached to you, let him be anathema" (Gal. 1:8). He is filled with anger when he denounces moral evils or the hypocrisy that pretends to a Christian attitude, or when he attacks the Jews, who seek to divide the Christians among themselves by cunning questions.

He knows that he has enemies and he is resolved to defend himself. But he cannot join to his resolve the same calmness and inner superiority which Jesus possessed in the Gospel. His attack is vigorous and passionate, and he points with pride to his own works and to the fact that the false Christians can produce nothing comparable. It must be admitted that, in not a few cases, his letters provide evidence of his training with the Pharisees. Sometimes the reader has difficulty in seeing the agreement of his writings with the simplicity of the Gospel. The Apostle called of the Lord was by no means free of a certain residue of all-too-human temperament, and was subject to influences derived from his educational limitations. He had become a "new man"; the persecutor had turned Apostle; but the past was still active in him, even if the human element was made subject to his calling. He suffered from the disadvantages attaching to his type of character and virtues. The passionate energy with which he dealt with his enemies is the reverse side of the intensity with which he took up the cause of the Lord, whom he had once persecuted. Joy and sorrow, love and anger, flow from his pen, and his letters are perhaps the most human documents of the ancient world. That his mission filled his whole personality is revealed in every sentence. Even the merest outsider was inevitably impressed by him, and by the manner in which the whole human being was permeated by the sense of his mission. One recalls his impressive conduct on board the vessel that took him as a prisoner to Rome (Acts 27:10). When all on board, including the sailors, lost their heads, he was the only man to keep calm and cool. When all were in despair, he encouraged them. He told them that he had been visited by an angel in the night, who had assured him that he would arrive safely in Rome, to appear before the Emperor. Through his manly courage, he saved not only his own life but the lives of all his fellow prisoners, since the soldiers guarding them had resolved to kill them rather than to risk their escape should the ship's company swim ashore after a wreck.

We must admire, above all, his genius for penetrating the minds and souls of others, which is revealed again and again. He is never afraid to speak openly of his temptations and sufferings, thus drawing very near to those who are a source of trouble to him. The strong personal note lifts his critical words above the level of a mere cold critique. He continually reminds his followers that he belongs to them, body and soul, and that he knows from his own experience all that they suffer. He is always thankful for good deeds done on his behalf, and he never fails to give utterance to his gratitude in words that move the heart. Speaking of the Epistle to the Philippians, a modern theologian says that it is a model of kindness, delicacy, and true heart-felt emotion: he adds that, "if our young people of today would trouble to get to know St. Paul, they would most certainly learn to love him" (Prof. Weinel, *St. Paul*, p. 290).

We can well understand that this man had real *friends*. This brings him very near to us; for, in friendship, humanity is made visible more clearly than in any other way and its higher values are made manifest. In his letters, he speaks of his fellow-workers in a manner so warm-hearted that it can spring only from genuine friendship. He calls Timothy his beloved and faithful son (1 Cor. 4:17). And, further: "Now if Timothy comes, see that he be with you without fear, for he works the work of the Lord just as I do" (1 Cor. 16:10). Even more moving are the words used in the Epistle to the Philippians (2:22): "But I know his worth: as child serves father, so he has served with me in spreading the gospel."

The reader naturally expects Paul to say that he had behaved as a father to the young apostle; but, by turning the relationship the other way round, he at once creates a situation in which the young apostle is drawn to his side in a friendly manner. Similar words of warmth and friendship are addressed to Titus, whom he calls his brother in recommending him to the Corinthians. Again and again, he places him side by side with himself as a comrade and fellow-worker (2 Cor. 8:22–23). He took thought even for the bodily welfare of his comrades and spared no effort to help them in case of need. This is clear from many passages in the letters.

But it would be unjust to imagine that the Apostle employed any unworthy means to secure the affections of the members of the Church. A marked degree of self-esteem is to be perceived in all his writings. To see this we need only examine the Epistles to the Corinthians and Galatians. He knows how to help make use of a biting irony, when he feels this will help to correct errors on the part of members of the flock. Yet, even if this irony caused some offense, we cannot justly accuse Paul of being arrogant or highhanded. He showed wonderful tact in dealing with Apollos, who had been chosen by a certain clique in Corinth to be their leader against Paul himself: he knew that Apollos had worked for the Gospel, and he gratefully recognized his services, even while defending himself against the formation of a dissident party.

It is not possible to define the specific humanity of St. Paul in a short sketch. His letters enable us to make our own picture of the true humanity in his make-up. He never denies it; he reveals it to the whole world, in the darker aspects as well as in the high lights. The most important apostle in early Church history stands before us as a *genuine man* with opponents and enemies; a man who could not—with all the good will of his followers—prevent misunderstandings and conflicts. Though, on the one hand, it cannot be doubted that numerous members of the groups he founded were conquered and brought into the fold by his deep humanity, love, and friendship; on the other hand, it is more than likely that many did not feel attracted by his personality and thus failed to find their way into the Church.

His openness in speaking of his troubles and triumphs is equalled by his candid exposure of difficulties and causes of offense within the communities. It is a grave matter when serious moral offenses are found in a community, following so closely upon the conversion to Christianity; for these early groups consisted wholly of converts. These men and women had been through a crisis, ending in an enthusiastic acceptance of the Gospel. Many of them had been compelled to undertake a radical revision of their mode of life in order to fit into a Christian Church. The Gospel should have been a source of grace and power to them. These early groups were touchstones for the virtue and efficacy of the new teaching. Yet how much room there was for improvement in these early communities; how much backsliding into the old paths of the pagan world! At first there were divisions: some declared for Paul, some for Apollos, others for Cephas, and a fourth group for Christ! Paul made use of all his eloquence in seeking to convince the members that both Apollos and he were no more than servants of God, entrusted with the mysteries of the Gospel and alike belonging wholly to Christ (1 Cor. 1–4).

Not only were there divisions, but these divisions were brought before secular judges: "Brother goes to law with brother and that before the unbelievers" (1 Cor. 6:6). Not understanding how to find reconciliation among themselves in Christian love, they made public the shame of the new communities.

Moreover, the difference between rich and poor, which should be overcome among Christians, is exhibited harshly even in the act of Communion (1 Cor. 11:20 sqq.). This act should be the expression of perfect unity in the love of Christ; yet it happens that one is hungry while another revels in wine. And, if this were not enough, Paul is forced to denounce unnatural vice among the Corinthians (1 Cor. 5). He would not have done this had it not been a source of open offense. He seems even to fear that the whole community might be infected by a few evil spirits: "a little leaven ferments the whole lump" (1 Cor. 5:6). He knows that, in the outside world, there are covetous men, extortioners and idolators, and knows also that the Christians cannot withdraw wholly from intercourse with such unless they leave the life of the world altogether (1 Cor. 5:10). But among the members themselves, so-called brothers, are to be found those who practice the same vices, and it is with these that a Christian should not share the table.

It would hardly be possible to speak more clearly about moral weaknesses in a community. He does not say that the elders or those who celebrated the sacred mysteries were themselves given to these evil practices; but in his reference to the Supper it is clear that causes of offense had crept into the liturgical fellowship itself; and these were of such a nature as to be in deep contradiction of the innermost meaning of the fellowship. This, at any rate, was the opinion of the Saint himself.

This early community demonstrates the fact that even the most spirited acceptance of the Gospel does not free men from their weaknesses and human passions; that, on the contrary, unceasing admonition and continual inner strengthening is neccessary in order to rise to the high demands of the Gospel.

Even if Paul did not bring his charges against the ministering officers of the communities, we can deduce, from the Apocalypse of St. John, that bishops in the early Church could forget their first enthusiasm and be untrue to their calling. "But I have a few things against thee, because thou hast some

The Human Element in the Early Church

there who hold the teaching of Balaam, who taught Balak to cast a stumbling-block before the children of Israel, that they might eat and commit fornication" (Apoc. 2:14). These words were addressed to the angel of the church in Pergamus. To the angel of the church in Sardis it was written: "I know thy works; thou hast the name of being alive, and thou art dead" (Apoc. 3:1). Of the Laodiceans, as is well-known, it was written: "I know thy works; thou art neither cold nor hot. I would that thou wert cold or hot. But because thou art lukewarm, and neither cold nor hot, I am about to vomit thee out of my mouth" (Apoc. 3:15–16).

It is thus seen that the Scriptures themselves provide a vivid picture of the early churches, leaving us in no doubt what the dangers were which then threatened—and *still* threaten. We are told that the Church is the Kingdom of God and the congregation of saints *upon this earth*, but that the separation of the wheat from the tares will not take place in this time or in this epoch, but only upon the day of judgment. The New Testament leaves us in no doubt that a conversion to Christianity is no guarantee that the vices of the world will not penetrate the Church itself or that the misuse of religion will become impossible.

The history of the early Church tells the same story. Again and again, members of the Church found a cause of offense in this all-too-human aspect of early Christianity—a reaction which, as we shall see, occurs frequently in later periods. It was unavoidable that, as the Christian communities grew in numbers, they would attract many whose moral strength was far from equal to the demands of the new life; such members, after a period of progress, were always liable to become backsliders. The history of the problem of repentance makes it clear that the struggle for a moral ideal continually occupied the minds of Church members. The early ecclesiastical writers, without exception, spoke quite openly of moral evils, and manifestly did not entertain the idea of a sinless body of Christians. The enumeration of sins and offenses demonstrates that, in many communities, the moral level was low. An early document (*The Shepherd of Hermas*) informs us that there were many sinners in the Roman Church who were guilty of grave moral evils. The writer mentions hot temper, adultery, drunkenness, slander, mendacity, avarice, deceit, etc. Certainly a quite comprehensive list of human failings! At the same time, we must not forget, the Church had to prevail against a host of enemies who had behind them the power and civilization of the world of those days.

The persecution was not constant and was carried through in different ways in different regions, the methods employed varying according to the attitude of the authorities. But, now here and now there, the attempt to put down the new religion was always active, at times taking on the form of attempted extermination by force. It is thus not surprising if many were prepared, under pressure, to deny their religion, more especially since the way was made easy for those who sought to escape the consequences. A simple gesture was enough to free an individual from the charge of hostility towards the state. He had merely to accept the worship of the Emperor in the accustomed form—not of course, allowed by the Church—or to betray his fellow Christians.

St. Paul himself demanded specific moral qualities from those appointed as bishops; these were indispensable. In the early centuries various ecclesiastical regulations laid down the moral and spiritual qualities which must be regarded as strictly essential in candidates for the office of bishop. The Church itself had the greatest interest in making sure that those selected for leading offices in the service of the Gospel

The Human Element in the Early Church

should be free from blemish, and thus likely to stand firm in the day of persecution.

This did not prevent some men of inferior calibre reaching the rank of bishop in the early Church: for example, the Bishop of Antioch, Paul of Samosata. History reports that certain bishops fell away during the persecution; and Cyprian of Carthage complained that a number of bishops left their flocks, went to outlying provinces, frequented markets and traded; he even charges them with avarice, with accumulating money and lending it out at exorbitant rates of interest (*De Lapsis*, 6). An outstanding scandal was the case of Novatian, a candidate for the office of bishop, who, by a trick, persuaded three bishops to travel to Rome and induced them, while under the influence of an excess of wine, to anoint him during the night.

With such facts before us, we perceive only too clearly that, though holiness was the task and aim of the Christian bodies, it was very far indeed from being attained during their pilgrimage on this earth. If, in these days, we find reports of many sins that seem peculiarly repugnant to later ages, the blame for this must not be placed upon the Gospel or the Church, but upon the age itself, whose children the sinners were. Given the sexual morality of the age, it was inevitable that sins of unchastity were very frequent. To assert that the stern moral demands of the Christian faith were responsible for these sins is to put the cart before the horse. Since the Christians came from an environment that saw no harm in many things condemned by the Church, it must have been particularly difficult for them to rise to the level of the new teaching. The more the ancient world sank into a decadent state, the more difficult became the task of the Church. The early Church confronted a decadent world with moral demands which, based upon perfection, could not be fulfilled.

It set up an ideal of holiness which must, of necessity, appear beyond attainment. Yet, through belief in this ideal, many sacrificed their blood and their lives. The ideal inspired heroic followers and for this reason it triumphed, in spite of every human weakness and imperfection. This struggle and victory can be pursued throughout the decline of the ancient world.

St. Augustine did not shrink from exposing his own sins and weaknesses in his *Confessions*. No one reading this work will maintain that this is done in any unworthy, objectionable, or tactless manner. On the contrary, the moral and religious spirit is so deep and earnest and the repentance so genuine that the darker aspects of the Saint's life, as described by himself, serve merely as a background throwing into bold relief the illumination of the great grace given to him. Most modern historians have recognized this. The Saint liberated himself from the pagan background of his earlier life; but, later, he made it clear what immense dangers had threatened him from this quarter. A bright light is thrown upon his age by the fact that this man, who made no attempt to conceal or excuse his sins and failings, was able to rule over his community with the most complete authority, leading it along the path of holiness. One is tempted to say: this period of history was honest and straightforward, compared with others which would certainly have found a cause of offense in the confessions of such a man as Augustine!

chapter 4 · What Is Essentially Human in the Church?

ONE may say that the answer to this question is simply: *human beings.*

This would signify that everything appertaining to man on this earthly pilgrimage is to be found in the Church. This statement can be taken in more than one way; and since the Church is a divine institution, the guardian of divine revelation, and the dispenser of divine mysteries, it is necessary to say precisely where the human element in the Church is to be found. It is seen not only in the persons and groups who form the Church here upon earth but in the institutions, laws and regulations, and in the hierarchical order.

When Christ founded His Church, He sought out apostles and followers who were given the task and the power to proclaim the Gospel to the whole world. He took them as men; and nowhere is it recorded that He promised them they would be supermen. He did not even promise that they would be outstanding men—save in the sense that an outstanding grace would be granted to them, and a renewal of spirit such as could be the gift of only a small circle of men. They remained human. They could not cast off their education, their racial character, their language, their personal idiosyncrasies, their good qualities or their failings. They grew up in a small, a very small world: a world in which the human and cultural ideas were the product, as we may be sure, of a small peasant civilization. Their language belonged to their age and their geographical situation, and this carried with it, as a language does, the mental and spiritual conceptions of a particular people.

They lived in an age characterized by one of the most important, perhaps the most important, melting processes known to history: namely, the fusing of original Greek conceptions, ideas, thought-systems, and institutions with Oriental and semi-Oriental ideas, manners, and customs. This period—the Hellenistic—lasted for several centuries. The apostles encountered on the highways Romans, latinized Greeks, and hellenized Jews. In Jerusalem at Easter they saw a vast conglomeration of peoples from all parts of the earth. All these things cannot have failed to make an impression upon their mentality, and must have played a part in their reception of the Word of God in the preaching of Jesus. The saying, later given a clear form in scholastic teaching, that grace always presupposes nature, is applicable to this situation. The grace of the Saviour alighted upon men who were changed by this grace—changed into followers of Jesus and children of the Kingdom of God, yet not destroyed in their nature, but lifted up, with the whole of their humanity, into another sphere. But, as this sphere was not visible, they appeared to their contemporaries in no way other than they were before, in their *human* aspect. Their sermons were delivered in their natural human speech, so as to be understood by their hearers. The Gospels, which they wrote primarily for the men and women of their time, could be written only in their accustomed speech, and they could use only the words in common use, the speech of the people, which was the one they commanded, by reason of their educational level and home environment. True, this speech was inspired, but this did not in any way weaken or destroy its human character: that remained, with all its significance.

The liturgy was celebrated in forms to which they were accustomed. They could not discover these forms for themselves even apart from the fact that the core of the liturgical life had been handed down to them from the Last Supper. St. Paul said: "For I myself have received from the Lord (what I also delivered to you), that . . . (1 Cor. 11:23).

That which he received he taught to his disciples and his congregations, making use of forms which, it is clear, had nothing extraordinary or unaccustomed for the period and for those whom he addressed. It would be quite childish to assume that the apostles had invented, on rational lines, new forms of liturgical life as if they were a Freemasons' Lodge. They were no more able to invent cultural and religious forms than to invent a new language. This applies to everything connected with religious worship and sermons, whether language, formal acts, or outward arrangements. It is very characteristic that the most significant elements in liturgical practices were wheat and wine, oil and water. These are required by man for the preservation of life and are adequate in themselves. These elements were sanctified in the various sacraments and used as instruments or vessels for the conveyance of grace.

The apostles entered the world of the hellenized Roman Empire as missionaries of the new faith—a world which at that time was virtually identical with the earth itself; for, in the minds of the Romans and the inhabitants of their realms, everything outside was looked upon, after the Greek pattern, as being summed up in one word: barbarism. It was thus inevitable that the civilization of this vast empire, speech, customs, legal forms, etc., should provide the earthly vessel for the wine of Christianity which the apostles brought to the world. Christianity in the early centuries found support in the traditions of the ancient world in the creation of its religious services and rites; it did the same with other forms of civilization. Many of these forms were so heavily burdened by pagan content that at first they were attacked by Christianity. Christianity took its first steps in a pagan world, but one that was not pagan as we understand the term today, but pagan in a pious sense. St. Paul said at Athens that the Athenians had a great fear of the gods. The actual Greek words could almost be translated in the sense that the Athenians were extremely, even anxiously, religious. Our modern concept of paganism carries a significance which in no way corresponds with the actual usage in the ancient world. The pagan world was completely permeated by religious concepts and forms. At the very root of hellenistic culture we find the Platonic idea of the symbolic nature of all earthly things, an idea which must undoubtedly have played a large part in the formation of cultural forms. Christianity could link up with this. On the other hand, all the forms of bourgeois life were so steeped in religion that, consciously or otherwise, men gave expression to some sort of religion through these forms. Hence the sharp struggle of the Christians against incense, against the theater, and against the cult of the Caesars. Considered for what they are in themselves, there are forms of a cultural type which can contain meanings of various sorts. Incense in itself is not a corrupt or evil thing; the theater is not in itself a pagan thing; reverence paid to the emperor has not in itself anything to do with a particular form of religion. We can thus understand that, as soon as the danger of a pagan significance attributed to them was over, many of the hitherto rejected and despised cultural forms were taken up by the Church, and, from then on, played a part in the formation of the liturgies.

What Is Essentially Human in the Church?

The human element in the Church consisted primarily in the people who represented the Church on this earth. As the Church penetrated one field of life after another, it experienced, of necessity, an influx of men and women of all kinds, of all classes, all races, and all characters. These people brought with them their racial peculiarities, their education, their cultural forms, their speech, and the ideals and purposes they bore within themselves, in a word, everything about them that was truly human!

The preaching of the Gospel was compelled to take into account the men and women for whom the revelation was intended. All these circumstances played their part in the development and history of the Church. When they preached to the Germanic tribes, the Christians gave the same message they had given to the Greeks and Romans, but on the one hand they adapted their language to the degree of understanding of the new race, and on the other the recipients took up the new religion with the human powers and special characteristics given them by God. When these new races had conquered and reformed the whole of the Western World, all the special qualities, both positive and negative, which distinguished them, flowed into the historical process shaping the Church.

When we study the history of ecclesiastical architecture, we are not at all surprised to find a development. Everyone knows that different styles of architecture arose in different centuries, that there were periods of high achievement and other periods when no marked changes occurred. This is still visible, and those who have eyes to see and have a certain training in the study of ancient edifices can easily perceive those developments. But how few are in a position to transfer the principle behind this process to other manifestations. It is self-evident that the Church took part, in all respects, in the cultural development of the West. Not only did it borrow from the ancient world even at the very time it fought against pagan culture but quite naturally was compelled, since it worked among men and women, to adopt the speech and forms of expression of the age and its peoples in order to carry on its work of leadership. The promulgation of the new revelation thus made use of the forms and means, proper to the humanity of the period, just as it made use of the people themselves. This did not prevent a mingling of dissimilar elements; this explains why the essential and the non-essential often combined together in men's minds. The Church maintained its claim not to insert new dogmas in the course of the history of dogma, even if the development of Christian dogma signified a visible progress in this history. If this be true, then it must be admitted that everything that is not direct dogma has been subjected in history to a real process of development. The assertion that the Church, of necessity, made use of the speech of the age, carries us further than would appear at first sight. To make use of a language means more than merely employing certain words as vehicles for thoughts and concepts. Some words possess a meaning and content the same in all languages—apart of course from certain refinements of meaning. Such terms as father, mother, son, or daughter, must in all languages carry the same essential content; even though certain emotional colorings attached to them may differ, the central significance does not change. But this does not apply to all concepts.

In the promulgation of the Gospel, the Church necessarily made use of certain concepts which, at the time of its entry into the world, already possessed special meanings. Such terms as God, spirit, salvation, savior, community, or Church were associated in the minds of men with a definite rational content and a firm concept. The words of the Gospel did not constitute a *system* in the philosophical sense of the term. Nevertheless, the words, deeds and whole life of Jesus were the elements out of which, in the course of time, the Church built up a system. The science of theology came into being within the Church. It was not handed by Jesus to the apostles as a ready-made gift, and passed on by them. It was given to be developed by human work and thought, by men within the Church and under the constant guidance of the Holy Spirit. But we must not forget that here the human element plays its part, a part that, throughout the progress of the Church and through the history of peoples, changes and must change. In spite of all the difference between peoples and races, the genuinely human will always remain the same as its core. If the Church, on entering the Western World, made use of certain intellectual systems that were anchored in the educational background of the then civilized world, we may well imagine that it often revised these systems to proclaim underlying truths in other languages, to make them more comprehensible to people brought up in wholly different world-concept. How difficult for example it must be for an East Asian to grasp the world-concept of the Middle Ages! The doctrine promulgated by the Church must be formulated, and these formulations must be firmly and definitely retained, even though the Church knows that, for example, the Divine Mystery cannot be wholly conceived in formulae, because it is immeasurably deeper and greater than human thought. The science of theology is entrusted with the task of penetrating even deeper into the revealed secret, employing all the means of human science and investigation. It is human if theologians attach a high value to formulations which will not have the same significance for a later age. It is the Church and the Church's *magisterium* that is infallible, and not the theologians, however important theology may be in the organic life of the Church.

The liturgy, considered apart from its dogmatic core, which naturally took its form at the very beginning, has in the course of centuries been developed, enriched and altered. Baptism as a sacrament handed down from Christ demands essentially the element of water, the act of baptism, or immersion, and the words accompanying it. Fundamentally this is a very simple process when we consider its importance and wide significance. One might indeed say that it is a matter-of-fact affair, since this baptism or immersion does not signify anything more than a washing. This very human process was selected by the Founder of the Church as the instrument of inward change when human beings were taken into the Church. We may regard it as being quite obvious that, given the feeling for form and the need for form which characterizes men—and more especially those of the ancient world—they would take this simple process in its various relationships, such as the casting off of the old paganism, the change to Christianity, the rejection of the past, and the pledging to a new life, analyze it and re-shape it. This applies to all the other sacraments and liturgical actions.

It is obvious that the outward clothing of the liturgy has undergone development, use being made of elements that had nothing to do with sacred things, things of a wholly profane nature! In all the various fields of civilization through which the Church made its pilgrimage, forms and elements were picked up. This applies to everything, save only that which was vitally concerned with the dogmatic core of the liturgy. But men and women are apt to regard as necessary and essential that which exists and has long existed, that to which they are accustomed. This can be seen in every department of life. It would be superfluous to refer to the political field, where it can be continually perceived that men look upon the disappearance of popular and cherished forms as signifying the end of the world.

The foregoing naturally applies to all the various departments of the life of the Church. The Church consists of living men and women; it exists for them and in no expression of its life can it deny the meaning and purpose of its existence. Because it is the Church of human beings, it must have a judicial order strictly appropriate to its aims and purposes. The forms which this order takes must be derived from the field of human life. When the Apostles went about preaching, they were compelled, in order to safeguard the position of the Church, to place bishops in charge of communities where such had been established. And when they themselves decided upon an area of permanent activity they had no alternative but to make some city known to them the center of their work. As the Church grew and spread, it became necessary to delimit and divide areas of work; and the obvious thing was to fit these into existing political divisions. To this very day we see in the word "diocese" the ancient term for an administrative area of a political nature.

The means adopted for the care of souls have changed; they will continue to change and must change. The Church of the martyrs used missionary methods very different from those of the modern Church; and it is certain that the Church in India will not achieve success with the means which might appear the only correct means to employ in the Europe of the twentieth century. Many will fail to distinguish between the human element in the care of souls and that which belongs to the essential and imperishable core of Christian faith.

Such practices as those of the pillar saints must seem quite incomprehensible to the Christian of today; even the most convinced of ascetically-minded Christians would not expect anything from similar practices today! But have we any more understanding for the practices of Indian penitents or of Buddhist monks? Yet to be successful, the preaching of the Gospel in India or in Tibet will have to adapt itself to forms which, to the inhabitants of these regions, are known as valid forms of expression for a true religious spirit. It would be a mark of plain stupidity to make a mockery of things we do not understand; the more stupid the man, the more he is sure of himself and contemptuous of others. It may be asked: how can we grant existence to such a crazy thing as the institution of the pillar saints? Yet in the field of so-called civilized life there are plenty of things in no way connected with religion, which are even more "crazy," even if they cannot be made use of against the Church! Every history of human civilization can supply an abundance of examples.

It is not possible to make it clear, in every concrete case, where and when the human element in the Church is essentially related to the supernatural. Visible order is a human thing. That there should be a visible order in the Church is an essential element in the life of the Church. Forms of expression are human. Yet it is vital to the liturgy that forms should be employed. Speech is changing and human, yet the proclamation of the Word cannot dispense with speech and will always make use of the language customary to a people at a given time. In one age it may speak more plainly, even more bluntly than in another when the sensibilities of a people compel them to make use of language to veil their thoughts. Abraham a Sancta Clara, the Augustinian friar, would be impossible today.* I am not sure whether or not this should be a cause of pride.

* Abraham was a Discalced Augustinian friar of 17th century Austria, noted for his eloquence. His manner of speech, though, would be quite unsuitable today.

In short, the Church is a divine institution. It came into the world to call men and nations to God. The gift it brings to men is of supernatural origin. The goal which it sets before men is not of this world. The men who came to the people on behalf of God and of Christ remained men, with all the characteristics proper to that state, including human inadequacy, weakness, and the possibility of corruption. The unchanging, imperishable element belongs solely to the divine in the Church. Infallibility has been bestowed upon the Church in the field of the Faith which it holds and propagates, and of the moral commandments. Just as good customs form a fence protecting morality, the truth proclaimed by the Church is surrounded by forms and customs. In proportion as men change, these forms and customs will be subject to change and development. There is nothing surprising if the tempo of the development of these forms and customs is different from that in the field of worldly affairs. For the former—even when they do not belong to the unchanging core—are bound up closely with the essential, unchanging and sacred. Why do we speak of ancient forms as "revered" or "honored"? Is it not remarkable that as a matter-of-course one associates reverence with age? Why do we find it natural that in the case of the Romans, for example, this or that cult should have been accompanied by rites that were a thousand years or more old? A novelist describing some historic religion would be certain to inform his readers that the priests employed forms of worship dating back thousands of years. We all realize clearly that in a general sense religious rites and forms are not subject to the same tempo of change and development as those associated with worldly matters. In the legal world also we can see how certain forms continue unchanged from century to century. We might say that wherever man lives a natural life—wherever he is not torn away from his natural roots and driven hither and thither by every sort of outward influence, as in our own age—the element of persistence is more important than that of change. It can happen that we cling to forms that we cannot understand or which have become devoid of meaning. It cannot be denied that many liturgical forms possessed at the time of their formation a meaning that was directly comprehensible. They arose from vital necessities and everyone could grasp the meaning from the form itself. When the bishop washed the oil off his hands after a confirmation or the ordaining of a priest, he performed a natural act, arising from the given circumstances, and making no demands upon the intelligence of the spectators. This natural act was later incorporated in the liturgy and became a part of it.

In the course of time, not only in the Catholic Church and its liturgy but in other public forms, the original conditions determining certain acts have ceased to exist, while the customs and rites have remained as they were in the beginning. This retention of forms, which at the present time can be understood only by reference to historical conditions, is justified because of the very close connection existing between the inner essence of the forms and the outward manifestations. It is, of course, possible to take the view that forms which cannot be understood save in this historical sense cannot, in the long run, be maintained, since it is not possible by reference to a historical development only to convince each new generation of the need for holding fast to venerable forms. This question is, however, linked with other problems which we propose to consider in another place. For this reason, we may return to the beginning of this discussion and say: the human element in the Church is that which emanates from men—the man himself and everything that he contributes to the gift of God. From these components, we obtain, in addition to all that is good, the various human weaknesses that we should prefer not to see in the Church. A man does not lay aside any of his essential characteristics when he becomes a Christian, even if he should be a bishop or the pope himself! He remains a man, exposed to all the usual temptations, as well as to the special temptations peculiar to the office which he holds.

There is another side to this question, and one that is too little considered. It was a part of God's plan of salvation that He should descend and become man, that His revelation should be clothed in the form of a human being, with human form and face, that, as messengers to the people, He should send not angels, nor theoretical teachers, but men of flesh and blood. Nay more—that it was His purpose to spread the Gospel more through the personal lives of His apostles than through their teachings. The Faith did not spread itself by means of intellectual argument, or the logic of apologetics, but, in a far greater degree, through the victorious logic of life itself. Men and women came forward to join the early Church because the apostles and martyrs, the preachers and the bishops, gave a living demonstration of salvation in their own persons; they were able to reveal themselves as converted and saved.* Christianity came to men and for this reason it spoke the language of mankind, fitted itself to human customs, and, coming into contact with new races and new types of civilization, incorporated much of the new in its formal presentation, and, above all, called upon representatives of the different races to be themselves responsible for the preaching of the Gospel to their own peoples. It would be a mistake to look upon the human element in the Church simply as a falling away from the divine idea, as a detraction from the Gospel message; it has quite another aspect—that of an incredible gift

* Compare the saying of Nietzsche. "His disciples must look to me like men who are saved." *Thus Spake Zarathustra*, Chapter 2. "Of Priests."

from God, taking pity upon us and going out to meet us in human form, not only through Christ but also through His Church. If we speak of men in the Church, that does not mean that we attribute to the Church the imperfections which characterize human beings.

"Certainly it is a degradation of a divine work to consider it under an earthly form; but it is no irreverence, since the Lord Himself, its Author and Owner, bore one also. Christianity differs from other religions and philosophies in what it has in addition to them; not in kind, but in origin; not in its nature, but in its personal characteristics; being informed and quickened by what is more than intellect, by a Divine Spirit. It is externally what the Apostle calls an 'earthen vessel,' being the religion of men. And, considered as such, it grows 'in wisdom and stature'; but the powers which it wields, and the words which proceed out of its mouth, attest its miraculous nativity." *

On the other hand, many moderns would suggest that there is a possibility of completely banishing the human element with all its failings from the domain of religious life by taking a right view of the true nature of religion. The modern age regards it as progressive to envisage religion as the most purely personal and individual department of human mental and cultural life. It was not by accident that Kant did not include religion within the scope of scientific study, and that Schleiermacher, a romantic among the theologians, characterized it as a subjective emotion. Emotions and feelings are, needless to say, outside control and cannot be regulated by laws.

Schleiermacher's conception of religion as primarily a specific emotion is, to a much greater degree than is usually recognized, an expression of the attitude of a period. It might appear that, through this philosophical standpoint, religion

* J. H. Newman—*An Essay on the Development of Christian Doctrine.*

would be firmly established and protected against attacks, by becoming an integral part of the soul of man, and thus of culture and civilization. In reality, however, it was thrust out of the general life of humanity and forced to take refuge in the least secure of all departments of life. The logical consequence of this theory is the phrase, "religion is a private affair," repeated so often by certain sections of the public in the nineteenth century. But who would not admit that religion is the innermost and most personal concern of each individual? Such an admission seems to lead to the conclusion that religion is a private affair, indeed, the most strictly private of all a man's affairs, a matter which he should not even speak about. The saying of Jesus that a man should enter into his room (see Matt. 6:6) to pray in secret, will not be forgotten in this connection, so that it might seem that even the New Testament approves of the doctrine of the purely inward character of religion.

Is not the fact that the Church has become a great institution, a vast social structure, not unlike the state itself, responsible for the weakness and inadequacy of the human element? On the other hand, if religion were to be brought back to the subjective world, as suggested by the school of Schleiermacher, if it became purely a relationship between the individual and God, so that the innermost core of the human being meets God, free from all outward forms, would not a whole series of stumbling blocks and difficulties be finally and completely removed at a single blow? It cannot be doubted that, since the age of rationalism, many have thought along these lines and that the number of those who sincerely cherish such convictions is still increasing. Even when individualism in other fields is rejected as false, it is held that, in the religious field, there is a genuine individualism, which is not only justified but even necessary.

Yet, despite all these arguments, whenever and wherever man has had real religion, it has always taken on an organized form. Even Buddhism, which intended to be no more than a guide to a happy life, a moral doctrine, developed with surprising rapidity into a sort of ecclesiastical system. It is intrinsically impossible that religion can remain an individual affair. Even an acceptance of the theory of Schleiermacher could not make it possible. If we take up the position that religion is an emotion, the situation is not altered; either it is a genuine emotion, or it is nothing. Every genuine emotion expresses itself in visible forms; even the most secret human love strives towards a visible expression. Even where feeling occupies the foreground, as in some branches of art, it is compelled to present itself in visible symbols and to bring its author together with other men, if only in the loosest form of organization, such as a group of friends or a "school." Moreover, the notion that religion is merely a matter of feeling or emotion cannot for a moment be accepted. Even if we entirely disregard Christianity, we must admit that religion as such is a concern of the whole man. It imparts to him a particular standpoint and outlook on life. A positive attitude towards religion means that a man no longer stands alone, and that his relationship to his fellow-men is different from that of the man who has no religion. The history of religion tells us that it always strives towards organization—or that a position is made for it within the community that is equivalent to an organization. Christianity is, however, a religion that was founded and given to the world by Christ. It claims that it came into the world in consequence of divine intervention and became a Church, not from its own desire or through some misunderstanding of the teaching of Jesus, but because it was the purpose of Jesus to establish His Church.

One thing we must not forget: when the Church came

upon the scene it stood for something entirely new and in the highest degree astonishing to the men of the age. They were accustomed to religion being an affair of the state, often important and highly valued, but all the same a part of the mechanism of the state. But the Church, from the beginning, claimed to be independent of the state and took upon itself straightway to declare that certain laws of the state were not reconcilable with man's conscience and were to be rejected; it took care to develop and guard this conscience, even when the heads of the state thought that they could disregard the scruples of individuals or groups within the state. The whole history of the West carries the stamp of this dualism. But the outstanding position of the West, with its vast importance in history, would not have been thinkable without this dualism; the Church gave to political life an undreamed of impetus and a host of new aims and purposes. The Middle Ages, with its prodigious achievements, was made possible through this bi-polarity. On the other hand, it gave rise to numerous possibilities of friction, which were derived, not so much from the principle itself, as from the fact that the servants of the Church, like those of the state, were human beings.

The servants of the Church, in every age, have been and are, for the most part, no more than average men, apt to be narrowed in their outlook by reason of their specialized work, as is the case with others who are compelled to limit their activity to tasks demanding entire devotion. Would one think any the worse of an artist because he regarded the problems of life from an artistic angle? This need not mean that he does not recognize the importance of other tasks, but that he does not value them in quite the same manner as do those whose special work they are. It is an obvious fact that the state official bears in mind the tasks assigned to him by the state: this is his duty. Even if he is a faithful member of a Church, he cannot forget this duty; he must always think of what will serve the state and enhance its prestige, unless this should go against his conscience. Such an attitude need not lead to conflicts; but conflicts can occur, for to defend the interests of a particular institution in a world consisting of imperfect human beings can always lead to some kind of collision. Every organization in the course of time acquires a certain position and this has to be defended and manned by human beings who, in their turn, come to possess rights, privileges and salaries—a state of things not always welcomed by other human beings. Yet who could expect the holders of such rights to give them up because others may regard them as out-of-date or useless?

In this way a number of conflicts are possible. Those who derive their positions and rights from some organization will be unwilling to admit that their work is no longer considered important. Least of all can this be expected from those whose work is religious, and linked with absolute ideas and beliefs, and even if the forms that clothe it are human and subject to changes imposed by time and the human element. Many examples can be taken from the history of the Church. It could hardly be maintained that the wealth of certain religious foundations, before the secularization of 1803, was used to further the Gospel teachings and to strengthen the Kingdom of God. This wealth was no longer fruitful in the sense intended by the founders; but the inheritors did not, in all probability, possess the spiritual power to create for themselves new tasks for the employment of the old resources. Such a state of things is not peculiar to ecclesiastical wealth; it applies to all important human foundations. Yet who could have expected those in charge of Church properties to give them up and see them devoted to other purposes, since they had every reason to look upon themselves as custodians and had actually taken a solemn oath to this effect? It is tragedy in the historical, as well as in the human sense, that is here revealed; a tragedy that no human power can remove from the world.

This is not the only case of a human tragedy in the Church. A trait which bears witness to human inadequacy and frailty, and is yet practically unavoidable, is the failure of Catholics to understand rightly those outside the Church. The Church has never failed to teach that the spirit of God blows where it wills, that the grace of God is not bound to the will of man. It teaches, accordingly, that every man of goodwill can come to the knowledge of God and attaches the greatest importance to *baptism by desire*. It knows further that the *logos spermatikos* of early Christian apologetics is effective in all religions: this means that genuine piety and love of God can be and is found in them. But it is easy to understand, although not easy to justify, that in practical religious life these facts are overlooked or at least given too little importance. It thus comes about that faithful members of the Church often acquire false ideas about the moral and religious position of those outside it. Many are well aware of St. Augustine's saying: "Many are outside who seem to be within; and many within who seem to be outside." It is hard for men to practice and keep before their minds the words of Jesus, spoken not alone for the Jews of His time but for every age: "Amen I say to you, the publicans and the harlots are entering the kingdom of God before you" (Matt. 21:31). There is no room for doubt in this saying. But it is human that it should so often be forgotten.

The relationship between the Church and the world of secular culture can also give rise to conflicts. The Church did not come to spread culture in the worldly sense, but to save souls. But, as a true religion, it gave rise to a great system of culture and was indeed for a time the sole bearer of culture and civilization. Later, by virtue of a natural process already to be seen in the Middle Ages, the various branches of culture separated themselves from the sphere of religion, and in some cases at least, served as vehicles of an anti-Christian outlook. If the responsible heads of the Church adopted a reserved and cautious policy towards many developments of culture regarded by the world as progressive, this merely shows that they were human beings! One of the most important of these developments was science, which has so often asserted the complete authority of its achievements, while charging the Church with being too slow in recognizing and adopting them. From a human viewpoint, it is understandable that the representatives of the Church were, at one time, too reserved with respect to genuine achievements in science and the arts. But, in view of the heavy responsibility they bore, we do not think that they can fairly be charged with excessive human frailty in this respect.

Chapter 5 · Perfection, Imperfection, and the Need for Reform

IN THE sacred books of the New Testament, the early Christians are frequently described as the community of saints. Those called to the new religion are the chosen, the beloved of God who have recognized the day of their salvation and are granted a certain expectation of the glory of the children of God. The Christians at all times, especially in the days of persecution, were inspired by a firm belief that the Lord would soon come to hold judgment. This held no terrors for the Christians, only for those who heard the call to repentance and paid no attention. It was joy and not fear that filled their minds when they looked forward to the Second Coming, the day of the glorification of the community of saints.

These beliefs must be kept in mind; also the fact that under the pressure of persecution and unceasing insecurity, eschatological hopes must have acquired exceptional power and made a most profound impression. But, while the communities thus awaited their returning Saviour, they had to carry on a struggle against the powers of darkness in this world, which never ceased to press their attack against the Kingdom of God. The goal towards which the Christian should strive was clearly defined by Jesus Himself. This high goal, He explained, was to become perfect, as God Himself is perfect. To be called to the Church signified to be called to the community of saints, to the company of the chosen, to perfection. To correspond with this a high moral level was essential, at least if the members took their calling seriously and cooperated in the work of grace. At the same time, the larger and more numerous the gatherings became, and the greater the reputation of the Church, the more attention was drawn to moral weaknesses and shortcomings incompatible with the high ideal of the one holy Church.

It soon became clear that the Kingdom of God was a gift demanding work and cooperation, discipline and self-denial. Was it not said in the Gospels (Matt. 11:12) that it could be taken only by violence? History provides the proof for the truth of this statement.

We must not seek to minimize the difficulties. Christianity came into the world in order to bring salvation. This salvation was given in the death and resurrection of Jesus. Paul did not say to his followers: "You will be saved." He said: "You are saved!" This was certainly an invisible grace: incorporation in the body of Christ brought about a mystical unity with the Lord. Yet at the same time this unity should bear fruits in this world. The task was to overcome sin and to set up an ideal of moral perfection.

But how can this come to pass if the Christian bodies were in no way different from those surrounding them? Among the heathen, too, there were many good and earnest men who sought after moral perfection. There were even some who, in a certain sense, embodied a human ideal. Together with these was the great mass of average men and women who were by no means outstanding in perfection, yet far from being notably bad. How did matters stand if the Christian community presented approximately the same picture? If, side by side with a number of genuine followers of Jesus, there was a far larger number of average people not strikingly different from the mass of unbelievers? Must salvation not be visibly revealed in the community?

Two factors in particular are often mentioned as making Christianity attractive to many heathens in the early days of the Church: a community spirit capable of overcoming everything; and the heroic martyrdom of many believers in the days of the persecution. Both express a strong victorious faith. In a worldly type of society, separatist interests usually prevent deep community feeling; but faith in the risen and returned Christ supplied a great future goal, which thrust otherwise natural interests into the background. Above all, the certainty of salvation was revealed in heroically endured martyrdom. These two factors continued to bring more and more recruits to the Christian communities. Most of these were average people, the children of their age. In these early centuries a great and courageous decision was not always necessary in order to join the new religion. At the beginning many went through a severe crisis before they came to the Christian Church, but as the communities grew larger this decision grew less difficult, although the fact remained that the Gospel itself demanded heroism from every follower of Christ. A Gospel that asks for perfection makes the greatest imaginable demands.

Nevertheless, the Gospel never stated that this demand would be fully and quickly fulfilled by all. Jesus Himself made it clear that the seed of the Word would not grow everywhere, that it would fall frequently upon stony soil or be choked by weeds, that the final separation of the good fruits from the weeds would not be accomplished until the Last Day. He left no room for doubt that the Kingdom would not be made known by direct success in this world but, on the contrary, what the children of this world call success would never be wholly given to the Kingdom. This does not alter the fact that He proclaimed salvation as a great gift given by God and held in readiness for man. Men of goodwill and open to receive grace are really saved, even though, in their condition of pilgrimage—*statu viatoris*—they can never be free from the struggle against evil, which they must seek to overcome in themselves and in the world.

Was the Church too accommodating, too willing to allow for the weaknesses of humanity in order to retain its followers? Did it not fit itself too smoothly into the ways of this world? Did it not create—even in the early centuries—a certain atmosphere of outward regularity and conformity which diverged widely from genuine inner repentance?

All these questions have in practice always been vital issues within the Church itself. There can be no Christianity without a certain measure of asceticism and flight from the world. This side of religious life may often sink into the background, as compared with the activity of the Church in the world, but it cannot and must not disappear. Whenever it has seemed that the Church had been swallowed up in worldly affairs the will to reform was born within the lap of the Church itself, again giving force to the other-worldly, ascetic tendency. The Church must be involved in a continual revolution, for the ideal of perfection perpetually demands new inner life and renewal. Religious life tends to crystallize itself into rigid forms and institutions, and these, in course of time, lose the force of their original ideals or even lose sight of them altogether: thus the will to reform is an essential characteristic of the Church of Christ. It is a fact, however, that the reform movements have often lost sight of their goal, turning the flight from the world into an end in itself, or, keeping alive the deathless Manichean heresy, they have denied the realm of nature as willed by God and thereby caused division in the Church.

Perfection, Imperfection, and the Need for Reform 53

During the first centuries of the Christian era there were alive movements which sought to attain, even in this life, the ultimate goal of the Church, the final realization of perfect sanctity. We have spoken of the conflict which raged over the repentance problem involving the delimitation of ideal and reality, of demand and fulfillment. Throughout the whole course of ecclesiastical history we find divisions due to the activities of over-zealous reformers aiming at immediate visible realization of the perfect holiness set as the ultimate goal. We can refer only to a few of these efforts.

As early as the second century we have the Montanists with their later follower Tertullian, who was at first a burning defender of the Church. The Montanists wanted to convert the last things (eschatology) into the present. The precondition of this was thought to be the introduction of a regimen that would be more ascetic than that of the orthodox Church. Hence the sharp rejection of second marriages, a stricter penitential discipline, special fasts, and, finally, a direct invitation to death through martyrdom. Tertullian's attitude is characteristic: adopting these views he denounced the condition of the Church as no longer corresponding with the evangelical ideal. This was the regular tactic of such movements: to set up a state of perfection, and urge its claims against the actual Church. Tertullian divided the Christians of his day into two groups: a lower, composed of the Psychists (called by him the loud-mouthed mass of the Psychists), and a higher group known as Pneumatics, described as possessing the true spirit. Thus Tertullian, in opposition to the words of Christ Himself (see Matt. 10:23) held the view that one should not flee persecution but allow himself to be taken with a view to securing martyrdom. He sought to forbid the remarriage of widows or widowers, to make the voluntary fasts compulsory, and to strengthen penitential disciplines. We find, again and again, that the penitential question played a large part, and especially the question whether certain sins should or should not be forgiven by the Church.

The fact of such reform movements within the Church is one of very great importance. It is true that the Montanist movement led away from the community of the Church and to the formation of a sect; nevertheless, reform in itself had a great significance for Christianity, indicating that the true crisis—crisis meaning decision—was a living issue in the community itself. This will to reform did not always assume forms leading to a break with the Church. St. Francis of Assisi was undoubtedly determined to reform Christian life, beginning with himself, then through his followers and, finally, through his example, working upon the body of the faithful. This will to reform is by no means confined to those ruling the Church; it arises frequently in the rank and file. It is characteristic of the Church as a living organism, and is of importance to every branch of the Church. The founders of great orders were often not priests, but laymen. St. Benedict went into seclusion not to be a priest, but to live a life of penitence. St. Francis was a simple layman, inspired by the Gospel and by his love of poverty to become an apostle. St. Ignatius, also, did not come from the priesthood, nor did he undertake his great works under ecclesiastical influence. But, all the great founders of orders, no matter what their origin, were inspired by an ideal of perfection, which they sought to make manifest for themselves and others. The Church knows, naturally, that men will always be imperfect and that it will not be made up of perfect men and women until the Last Day. Nevertheless, it is the duty of the Church to preach perfection, and to fulfil the command of Christ, which demands of men that they should become perfect.

It is easy to understand that this commandment of Christ

can be misunderstood and perfection be demanded not only as an ideal but as an immediate reality in the present. When the reformers attacked the "spirit of the world" that had entered into the Church, they took the stern teachings of the Gospel as their point of departure. The reforming spirit, whether destructive or constructive, was kept alive during the Middle Ages. To arrive at a just judgment we must bear in mind both of these types, side by side. Reforms in the orders and the founding of new orders come into these categories. Even the extremists were of importance for the Church. For example, Arnold of Brescia, in the twelfth century, preached with passion against the secularization and demoralization of his age. He called attention to the poverty of Christ and denounced the gross contradiction between the Church and the Gospel. Remarkably enough, it was those belonging to the well-to-do bourgeois circles who flocked to him. Encouraged by his success, he increased his ascetic demands to the point of complete Utopianism.

A similar movement was that of the Albigensians in the south of France. The heresy of the Cathari was also based upon the contradiction existing between the asceticism of early Christianity and the rigid social system of the Middle Ages when at its height. The Cathari claimed to live the life of Christ and His apostles. They called themselves perfect and asserted that nothing imperfect should be allowed within the Church. The power and possessions of the Church were singled out in attack, and the decadence of the age was put down to these causes. It is interesting to note that preaching against these heretics did not meet with success until Bishop Diego of Huesca entered upon a preaching pilgrimage in apostolic poverty.

Let us consider Wycliff, who also protested, in the first

place, against the worldliness of the Church and the clergy. He wished to abolish every sort of worldly power and authority on the part of the Church. He believed that the "Donation of Constantine" was the fount of all the evil and held the view that the state should liberate the Church from these things. He took his stand upon the Gospel teaching. But as the struggle progressed, dogma was drawn into it as well as politics. He wanted to establish an organization of priests living in apostolic poverty and setting an example to the people. But it was not long before he attacked vitally important dogmas and institutions of the Church: the receiving of the sacraments, the hierarchy, transubstantiation, the veneration of the saints, etc. The reform movement of Professor Huss of Prague was doubtless derived from the Wycliffian source. It should be remembered that even those movements that led to a falling away from the Church and the setting up of sects, however deplorable they may have been, were, in the first instance, often a genuine expression of a desire for perfection existing in the Church itself. Even when they failed in their purpose, they were not without importance for the Church and its renewal. Ecclesiastical historians have more than once pointed out that the Catholic Church gained an unforeseeable and quite unexpected new impetus as a result of the Reformation and its fight against Protestantism. Indeed we cannot deny that a falling away from the Church is in itself a serious sermon on repentance. We human beings have no right to discuss the question of moral guilt in the case of those who caused disruption in the Church and distribute blame to the various persons concerned. That is wholly a matter for the Supreme Judge, from whose eyes even the most secret thoughts cannot be hidden.

The Church may establish the objective guilt of those who

Perfection, Imperfection, and the Need for Reform

thus left the Church; but it does not in any way deny the guilt of those who remained in the Church, who by failing to observe the commands of the Gospel were themselves partners in the offense and disloyalty of the seceders. It is human that, in the struggle for renewal, human logic and love of conflict should play a rôle embittering men's minds and forcing them apart, instead of bringing them together. If the struggle then assumes the form of a conflict between political parties, this also is a manifestation of human weakness. It would not be possible to maintain that the struggle between the denominations was, at all times, such as to bring honor to Christianity! However, it is not the fault of Christianity if it is led by men who have no desire to build up, as the Apostle said, but fight from merely human motives or even for the sake of the struggle itself. During the last century, the conflict between the denominations was often carried on by men who took no interest whatever in saving souls. For such human political aims it would not be fair to hold the Church or the Gospel responsible.

In the history of the Church there has been hardly a single century when genuine reformist ideals did not seek to prevail. We cannot be surprised if an equal number of less genuine movements raised their heads. It is, however, a natural human reaction if reformist ideals are felt to be uncomfortable and, for this reason, to be put down as false and unjustified. As might be expected, the various reforms in the lives of the orders, demanded from time to time, did not always meet with a good reception from the representatives of the orders. Since the Church and its institutions are apt to cling to established things, it is frequently to be seen in ecclesiastical history that those who put forward reforms were faced with the charge of being innovators—the term being used in such a manner as to bring it very near to the more dangerous term, heresy. This is a very human reaction; for to cling to that which has been proved of value is as necessary as to reform what is no longer of value. There will always be a struggle in the Church against secularization, and an appeal will always be made to the Gospels.

Since the Church is in the world, it will always bring forth institutions which are *human*, acting as earthly vessels devoted to a divine purpose; therefore the possibility of a deterioration of these institutions can never be ruled out. In the same way, the most perfect political institutions evolved by the most penetrating minds cannot be prevented from suffering decay. Ecclesiastical institutions—unless they rest upon direct divine intervention—cannot be removed from a liability to decay and corruption. For this reason, self-examination, renewal, and reform must always find a place within the Church.

It can never be denied that Christians should become perfect. Even in the secular field, human education must aim at an ideal, at an unattainable state of perfection. The recognition of moral ideals lies at the root of all moral effort and the tragedy of human life is revealed in this effort; for men and women must have a positive goal which they recognize and towards which they strive, but which they know they can never wholly achieve. How much more must this tragedy, which is a part of the inheritance of fallen and sinful men, be apparent in the Christian community? The Church knows the mystery of iniquity and, despite all modern assertions to the contrary, it knows better than those outside it think the true depth and tragedy of this mystery: namely, that the grace of salvation may not be understood and be rejected or even misused by humanity. Beyond this, it knows—this is a dogma —that divine perfection is an unattainable ideal, infinitely beyond and above all human thought and comprehension. Yet Jesus gave utterance to His greatest commandment, embracing all the others, when He said to His disciples (Matt. 5:48): "You therefore are to be perfect, even as your heavenly Father is perfect."

Chapter 6 · Temptation Through Power

THE legend of the Grand Inquisitor is well-known, and has frequently been commented upon. It seeks to demonstrate in a striking picture the nature of the deep offense given by the western Church, especially in the Middle Ages, to those circles antagonistic to the Church. The question is asked: has not this Church become the incarnation of power, in place of being the instrument of the Gospel of poverty? Has it not been conquered by the third temptation—the achievement of worldly power?

Let us briefly consider this legend, as it is described in Dostoievsky's great novel: *The Brothers Karamazow*. Christ has lived and proclaimed His Gospel, and promised to return as judge. There were many who followed Him, but Satan was not idle. Doubt spread among men and all manner of sects arose: in short, humanity pursued a path far removed from the true doctrine of salvation. Thus, at the end of fifteen centuries, men yearned more than ever for a Saviour. Then in His mercy He resolves to appear, if only for a brief moment, among "the tortured, suffering and sinful people" who nevertheless loved Him in a childlike manner. The author places this appearance in Seville at a time when the Inquisition was most terrible, when, as he puts it, piles of bodies sent their smoke rising up to Heaven in praise of God. Naturally, Christ does not appear among the people as judge—that had been promised for the Last Day—but in the same simple human form that He had assumed before. Nevertheless, everybody recognizes Him. An irresistible power draws them and He is followed wherever He goes. With a smile of infinite pity He wanders silently among the crowds. Power and salvation radiate from Him, causing those near Him to quiver with love. He is surrounded with healing power. He again performs miracles: the sick are healed and a dead child is restored to life, just as the body is being taken out of the cathedral. At this very moment the Grand Inquisitor passes by. He is a vigorous old cardinal of ninety years; in his wrinkled face the sunken eyes gleam with a terrible fire. He wears his rough monkish habit and his assistants follow at a discreet distance.

In an instant he realizes the whole situation. He frowns and his gaze is maleficent. He orders the guards about him to seize Him. So great is his power that the people dare not oppose him. They kneel and the Inquisitor blesses the crowd, while Jesus is led to a narrow cell in the palace of the Tribunal. In the middle of the night the Inquisitor comes to Him and says: "Art Thou the Man?" He does not wait for a reply but adds: "Do not answer, keep silent! What couldst Thou say——? Thou hast not even the right to add anything to what Thou hast said before!" Continuing, the Inquisitor accuses Him of coming to disturb the existing order. But he, the Inquisitor, will judge Him and cause Him to be burned as a heretic of the deepest dye. Jesus makes no answer.

Dostoievsky's own comment is to the effect that the fundamental feature of Catholicism is the handing over of moral and religious responsibility to the pope; Jesus Himself gave up the keys and installed the pope as His representative. Therefore, so Dostoievsky thinks, the Inquisitor was justified in demanding of Jesus that He should not interfere with the established order; He has no right even to reveal anything appertaining to the spiritual world from which He descended. For thus freedom of conscience, once so dear to Him, would be destroyed, the same freedom taken away by the Church in order to secure the happiness of the people. The result of fifteen hundred years of work is that men have not been able to bear the weight of a freedom of choice between good and evil, and have laid it at the feet of the Church. In the three temptations, Christ was warned. But He rejected the suggestion to give bread to the people, because He feared that in this way they would lose their freedom. He should first have fed them and then demanded virtue from them. For never, says the Inquisitor, will they be able to feed themselves by their own powers. No science can give them bread, as long as they retain freedom; and thus it will end in their bringing their freedom to us and saying: "Make slaves of us; but give us enough to eat!" They will learn finally that freedom is incompatible with a sufficiency of food, for never will they understand how to divide among themselves. It is therefore essential that a few should have responsibility and the burden of freedom in order that the masses should have bread. Men do not want freedom; they want to find someone who will rule over them. They will always render allegiance to those who give them bread. Freedom of choice between good and evil, on the other hand, will always be rejected by the masses. They will prefer death itself. Christ demanded a free gift of love from the people and in this very way He increased immeasurably their spiritual sufferings, leaving them in a worse state of confusion than that in which He found them. The Inquisitor told Jesus that He had overestimated the possibilities of humanity, in putting forward the ideal of love freely given. "Men are slaves. Look about Thee! How many have risen to Thy level? Men are far lower and weaker than Thou hast believed." Therefore, a few bold men willing to bear freedom have seized power by force and taken freedom away from the masses, thus doing what Christ should have done Himself! These few did not find happiness for themselves; but they brought it to others.

The attack of Dostoievsky is here directed against the Roman Catholic Church, and more particularly the Church in the Middle Ages, for he hated the Church as much as he hated German civilization. His charge against the Church was in the main based upon the conviction that the masses cannot bear the responsibility of moral freedom. But Jesus called upon men to be free spirits, thus placing upon their shoulders a burden they could never carry. The Tempter understood human nature better than did Jesus, and warned Him that the masses must be fed, compelled to conviction, and led by authority. This was understood by the Church in the Middle Ages. That is the inner meaning of the development of the Church: it leads the people with authority, makes their decisions for them, takes away their sins, and thus, through its power to forgive sins, enables the people to go on sinning.

The charges brought against the Church in the Middle Ages are not all of so basic a character as those put forward by Dostoievsky and voiced by the Grand Inquisitor. The Church has been disfigured by many human weaknesses in the course of the centuries; nor can it be denied that these were both numerous and serious at certain periods. The Church is not interested in concealing historical truths. What Berdyaev wrote in 1935 in his book, *The Destiny of Man*, is not true: "The whole of the Roman Catholic account of Papacy is based upon conventional lies and falsifications which serve to create the myth of Papalism." *

The problem is quite simple. Has the Church really been

---

* N. Berdyaev—*The Destiny of Man*, p. 207.

conquered by the three temptations, and thus reversed the true teaching of Christ? The moral conduct of individual popes, for example, is a matter of secondary importance. The Middle Ages had many dark aspects and the Church was not free from them. But we must not forget that we are here dealing with an immense space of time, no less than a thousand years! It would be a cause of rejoicing among Catholics were they able to point to the long list of popes and say: "Yes, all of them were saints!" But the very nature of the Church makes such a miracle impossible. The popes held an extraordinary office, but they were not always extraordinary men. In fact, the unique importance of their position was a chief reason why the human element was peculiarly likely to make itself felt. For, firstly moral and then political power were bound up with the papacy. It cannot be demonstrated that the popes sought political power and conquered it by human means; but we see throughout history that a moral power may give rise to a political power. The great power over the minds of men wielded by the papacy was, in itself, sufficient to bring with it political power. That secular rulers should seek to make use of the papacy for their own ends goes without saying. In the Middle Ages the personality of the pope was of the highest importance to secular powers. It followed that these powers endeavored to influence the election of the pope and his policies. The fact that power-political factors operated in this way cannot fairly be laid at the door of the papacy itself, which was able to exist, as history has shown, without political power. But it is not difficult to perceive that, given the conditions then obtaining, there is nothing surprising in the phenomenon of ambitious men pushing themselves forward, or being pushed forward, in the direction of the papacy. There has never been a period in history when the misuse of power did not constitute a difficult problem and no effective means of preventing such misuse has ever been devised.

Certainly we know that the Church is guided by the Holy Spirit, but it is a painful fact that this has not prevented the highest office in the Church being, at times, abused and dragged through the mud by its occupants. It must be understood that the spirit of Christ which guides the Church is not exhibited solely in the person who may at any given time occupy the throne of the papacy; it dwells within the body of the Church. Bearing all these facts in mind it is somewhat remarkable that not one of the Bishops of Rome ever made an attempt to convert his dominion into a purely secular power as would certainly have been possible at more than one time. Nor should we forget that the moral weaknesses and sins to which we refer are concerned with a very small section of the long list of popes, and that many of them are remembered for great and splendid deeds. Popes, like other men, are human beings and therefore open to every kind of temptation; they need the spirit of divine grace as much as other Christians. None of them can claim, or ever has claimed to be free from sin.

The second temptation of Christ would have been truly successful had all popes been outstanding saints, for this would be a miracle so startling as to wipe out all doubt! The popes who failed to live up to what was called for in their lives as Christian leaders were a reproach to their age rather than to the Church. The various writers and journalists eager to discover unsavory details discrediting the papacy would find a far greater abuse of power and privilege if they turned their attention to the archives of the secular powers. It is accordingly meaningless to deal in detail with the scandals and offenses that have been dragged into the limelight. The little democrats who consider themselves able to sit in judgment upon the popes must be called upon to prove that their own moral standards and conduct would have been better than those of say, Alexander the Sixth, had they enjoyed the same extent of power and privilege. There are many literary men who act as if they had only just discovered Alexander the Sixth, and felt themselves bound to reveal to Catholics facts of which it is assumed they are in total ignorance. Yet, when this pope ruled in Rome, it was no secret that Caesar and Lucretia Borgia were his children. The whole Catholic world has known for centuries far more about the "wicked pope" than is known to the half-baked critics of modern times! Moreover, the world of the Faith has suffered more deeply from these things than from attacks from the outside without for a moment losing its heartfelt belief in Christianity as the highest Good, because its faith has never been placed in man, least of all in a prince of the renaissance, but in God.

The question put by the Grand Inquisitor is of a far more essential character: namely, did the Church seize power in order to take away responsibility from the people, and thus rule over them with absolute authority? In the first place it must be established that Dostoievsky gives a false picture of the essential message of the Gospels. Jesus did not proclaim a Gospel for a few chosen spirits, and His demands were not such that only a few such spirits could hope to fulfil them. But an overcoming of the natural man was certainly demanded, a demand that did not signify following the line of least resistance. Jesus knew well that most men would prefer the broad way to the narrow path that leads upwards, and that a too strong attachment to the things of this earth stands in the way of Christianity. How difficult it is for a rich man to enter the Kingdom! He knew the strength of the ties holding men down to the earth and He pointed out again and again that these ties must be loosened. Yet it was to the people that He brought His Gospel. He understood that the common people are less hemmed in by such ties than those higher up in the social scale, and much less than those who are filled with self-sufficiency and pride. The only sin that excludes men from the Kingdom is the sin against the Holy Spirit. Jesus knew that the poor and despised are often more open to spiritual truth than the occupants of the seats of the mighty. The majority of those who followed Him were quite ordinary men and women. He asked nothing of them, save that they should believe in Him with heart and soul. It cannot be said that the disciples of whom we read in the Gospels were outstanding characters. Christ knew the instability of the masses, how quickly they can be aroused to enthusiasm—through bread—and how rapidly they can swing round.

But in spite of everything He came to take pity on the people. The Church on its part has always held fast to its sacred mission: to proclaim the Gospel to the people as a whole.

In the Middle Ages a decision for or against the Church was requested from every individual. This involved for every man and woman, as must always be the case within a Christian community, a fundamental direction of life towards holiness and a high ideal of perfection. But since the majority of people, in every age, are no more than average, this acceptance of Christian ideals is far from signifying that the average man becomes a saint. The Church has never taken responsibility away from the individual, even from the simplest man of the people, although it explains the application of the Gospel teaching in concrete cases, aiding the individual to discover the voice of his own conscience. But the Church has never abandoned the basic principle that the final subjective instance for each man is his own conscience. The fact that many Christians prefer to rely upon concrete directives rather than on their consciences does not in any way affect the teaching of the Church upon this matter. We are apt to confuse pressure exerted by society upon men and women with the teaching of the Church. The fact of being placed in a particular society relieves the individual of the burden of a number of decisions, since by custom he is wont to accept certain lines of conduct. A large number of our moral decisions are in reality formed for us. In a society steeped in faith like that of the Middle Ages it is very difficult to declare oneself as standing apart from the life of faith. But it should not be concluded from this fact that freedom of the individual is destroyed. In a society where there is little faith it may be just as difficult to declare oneself a believer. In this case many become unbelievers through cowardice or in mere imitation. Nevertheless, those who despite their better knowledge are unable to decide for belief in such a position cannot be held, as the Apostle said, free of guilt. If there are men and women who hold to the faith of the Church out of cowardice, inertia, or through mere custom that does not prove that freedom of decision has been taken away from them.

The forcible means often employed in the Middle Ages were derived to a greater degree from the desire to protct society than from the desire to protect the Church, more especially when force was used against those who threatened the political and social order as well as the unity of the Church. This emerged with special clarity in the case of the Spanish Inquisition which was as much concerned with the protection of the people and the social order as with the unity of the Church. The power of the Inquisition was doubtlessly abused, but we should not forget that abuse of power is general and comes under the head of human weakness. The Inquisition and its methods and cruelties cannot be judged justly, save against the general background of the Middle

Temptation Through Power

Ages and the prevailing legal practices. An age in which a whole society is filled with enthusiasm for a high and exceptional goal will always make use of protective measures of a different kind from those employed in a society devoid of ideals. This is one of the tragedies of human society: namely, that on the path towards a high ideal men create not only good but also evil.

To return to the question of moral conditions among the clergy in the Middle Ages. It would be an error to draw general conclusions as to the Church itself from special cases among popes and bishops. In condemning justly such cases—for example, certain renaissance popes—let us not forget that at this very time the Church was able to produce a number of outstanding saints. It is a bounden duty to point out that in the reign of Alexander the Sixth the Gospel working in the Christian community gave rise to fruits of holiness of an exceptional nature, sometimes in the shadow of the palaces of men whose lives made a mockery of Christ's teaching. We are compelled to doubt the sincerity of those who concentrate exclusively upon the dark aspects of an age and ignore the bright light which shone forth at the same time from within the Church itself.

It must strike an impartial critic that the people, who were perfectly well aware of the failings of the popes in question (note Dante), did not allow themselves to be led astray, but continued to practice a strong religious life. Nay more: at this very time and among this very people a number of saintly men arose who exhibited in word and writings an inwardness of spirit, a separation from the things of this world, and a unity with the life of Christ that can serve as a model for every age. If a table were to be drawn up showing, on one side, the names of all those whose conduct gave the most offense and, on the other, a list of those who did the most to promote the Gospel, the second column would be seen, despite everything, to outbalance the first. When we have said all that is necessary to express our disapproval of the historical figures who gave offense, we can place on record the fact that these human weaknesses help us to perceive in their true light the essence of the Christian Faith and the Church. The men who held the guiding reins in their hands were no gods or supermen as the legend of the Grand Inquisitor suggests, but men like all other men, even if they were called to the lofty task of acting as representatives of Christ and proclaimers of the Gospel. Had they actually been gods they might have made more impression upon men's minds.

Even when deprived of all secular power the pope remains a powerful factor in the scheme of things, since he represents for many millions of people the highest authority in the most important sphere of life. For this very reason it is much to be desired from a human standpoint that this authority should be secured in its independence and not allowed to become a piece on the political chessboard. When a moral authority of the first rank is placed in a world of conflicting political forces, it is inevitable that these forces will seek to make use of the moral power. For this reason the popes insisted upon guarantees of political independence. Pius the Eleventh, who succeeded in restoring complete independence to the Holy See also in external affairs, expressed the importance of this sovereignty in a very notable and beautiful manner: "We would view things from the standpoint of the blessed St. Francis; just enough to keep the body united to the soul. . . . The Supreme Pontiff has possession of no more material territory than is absolutely necessary for the exercise of the spiritual power entrusted to men for the benefit of men. We have no hesitation in saying We are well pleased that things are thus. We rejoice to see the material earth reduced to the min-

Temptation Through Power

imum term which can and ought to be spiritualized by the immense, sublime and verily divine spirituality which it is destined to sustain and serve."

Maritain comments upon this: what is here said by the pope is at the same time a symbol for the entire order of temporal things seen as instruments of the spirit; and (he continues) we may permit ourselves in respect of this order to be wholly optimistic.

The words of the pope make it clear that the Church lays no claim to worldly power, most certainly to no power going beyond that which is absolutely necessary to secure the liberty of the Church within its proper sphere. It is, however, human that the faithful should continually seek to surround its vast spiritual authority with a certain protective secular authority.

chapter 7 · Changes in the Position of the Clergy

THE position of the clergy in relation to the people has undergone changes down the centuries. These do not affect the fundamental nature of priesthood, but they have importance for the growth of the Church and the proclamation of the Gospel, as the social and psychological conditions determining the acceptance of the Gospel at each stage of development cannot be disregarded. It is not possible to show in any detail how these relationships between clergy and people with all their actions and reactions developed through the ages.

In a Christian community consisting mainly or even wholly of men and women who had found their way to the Christian faith through struggles and inner crises and who elected from their midst their priests and leaders it is clear that the relationship between the members and those who acted as dispensers of the sacred mysteries must have been of a kind very different from what we know in our own age. In the days of early Christianity such conditions actually obtained. Only men and women who had been through struggles of a more or less revolutionary character demanding the utmost personal effort came to Church at all. Their attendance was a profoundly important personal decision. For such people the Church was the hidden treasure, the pearl without price for which they were ready to sacrifice all—even life itself. We cannot find any words to describe what this must have signified for the religious and social life of these men and women. One thing is certain: the Church was their concern, their own peculiar interest; it was the affair of each one and of all. Going to church as a matter of form on the part of those who inwardly stood aloof was a state of things barely conceivable. It was a case of either-or: one belonged to the Church with heart and soul or one stood outside. The priests in these communities had been through the same struggles as the members. It is true that they were appointed by the apostles, but they came from among the community or were elected by the community; they came in any case from the narrow circle of the faithful. A relationship of great confidence and trust on the part of the flock towards the shepherd must have existed from the very beginning, although this did not exclude the possibility of a change in such relationship if needful. The shepherd did not always prove worthy of confidence or he may himself have failed in firm faith; such happenings were not rare. But the basic relationship itself did not depend upon individual circumstances, but always upon the spirit of the whole and upon the dominant factors in the sociological pattern.

When Christianity became the recognized religion of the Roman Empire, the Church was still very far from having conquered the field of culture. Roman culture had obtained a certain footing in the Church, but in the towns the Christians were to be found among the lower classes and the poorer middle-class, while in the country they very often came from a peasant population which was virtually untouched by culture. The power of the middle-class official and executive order suffered decay in the latter days of the Empire through the growth of a top-heavy bureaucracy, and this fact aided the development of Christianity. Christopher Dawson points out in his work *The Making of Europe:* "The office of the bishop was indeed the vital institution of the new epoch. He wielded almost unlimited power in his diocese, he was surrounded by an aura of supernatural prestige and yet, at the same time, his was an essentially popular authority since it sprang from the free choice of the people. Moreover, in addition to his religious authority and his prestige as a representative of the people, he possessed recognized powers of jurisdiction not only over his clergy and the property of the Church but as a judge and arbitrator in all cases in which his decision was invoked, even though the case had already been brought before a secular court. Consequently the episcopate was the one power in the later Empire capable of counter-balancing and resisting the all-pervading tyranny of the imperial bureaucracy. Even the most arrogant official feared to touch a bishop and there are numerous instances of episcopal intervention not only on behalf of the rights of individuals, but also of those of cities and provinces" (p. 28).

The relationship between the bishop and his flock could not fail to be changed following upon these profound alterations in status, even if his first and most important tasks were essentially of a permanent nature. The bishop now stepped outside his original function of spiritual shepherd and became at the same time a power in public life. The dangers surrounding his life and work were obviously greater. It would seem probable that the personal relationship between bishop and flock would in some respects at least become more distant. On the other hand nothing could prevent a steady growth in the power of the bishops during the early Middle Ages, since the office of bishop was the only unchanging position of importance within a world of ever-shifting political changes and upheavals. Princes and barons might come and go; lands might be conquered or lost; but dioceses and parishes remained. The

Changes in the Position of the Clergy

people realized that the bishops were the most secure support in an insecure world.

Quite another picture is presented at the height of the Middle Ages, when the Church stood at the summit of its power. It has always been the case that social patterns have rested upon the bases of philosophical principles. At this period the Christian religion dominated this world concept of the entire western world. The Christian view of this life and of the next world had so completely taken possession of men's minds that it was accepted on every hand as a matter of course and outside criticism. The Church was the unchallenged leader in certain spheres of life. The fields of science and art could be entered only through the gates of the Church. The monasteries were the special guardians of learning. The universities in their early days, when they took over much of the work of the monasteries, were ecclesiastical institutions. Even as late as 1840, the two universities which had cherished most faithfully the mediaeval pattern, Oxford and Cambridge, were still, properly speaking, clerical bodies. As the men of the Middle Ages became more conscious of the importance of science and knowledge in general and enthusiastic disciples flocked from every land to Paris, Bologna, or Salerno, it was taken for granted that the universities should derive their sanctions from Christian authorities, from the pope or the emperor or both. The word *clericus* acquired a special sense, denoting the man who alone possessed the right to occupy himself with knowledge and learning.

The privileged position of the clergy in the cultural world drew numerous men of all nations not only to the universities but into the ranks of the clergy where many sought to enter without any idea of ever becoming priests. Naturally the priesthood itself continued to exist and function, but it took on a different appearance and acquired a greater influence; it grew into the most important social power. At the same time the wealth and secular power of the bishops and of the monasteries greatly increased. Side by side with this there grew up gradually in the towns an independent bourgeoisie, bringing with it another type of social order. It followed that a certain rivalry and opposition came into being between these two patterns of life, but all this took place under the wing of the Church and the people experienced this development without being aware of any opposition to the spiritual order. Furthermore, various organizations and social processes now helped to bring into the foreground the importance of lay elements within the Church.

The growth of the guild system was accompanied on the ecclesiastical side by an expansion of the religious brotherhoods. Some movements such as the begging orders rested upon a wide popular support. The founding of these orders has been not unjustly described as a democratic movement inside the Church. The question of ecclesiastical privileges, especially in regard to taxation, gave rise, not unnaturally, to serious conflicts between the "people" and the clergy. But not until after the period of the Reformation did these lead to actual breaches with the Church. For centuries the conception of the Church and its growth as an affair of the whole people had permeated the consciousness of men and women and for this very reason they were free to occupy themselves with the failings and human weaknesses of the clergy. Sarcasm and mockery were the recognized weapons in attacks against immorality, abuses, and every sort of inadequacy in the ranks of the clergy. Nobody raised objection to this form of criticism, since neither the Church as such nor the clergy were challenged fundamentally. It is quite characteristic that the figure of Till Eulenspiegel, so well known in the Middle Ages, was actually given real life in the person of the priest, Amis, who managed to get his own way in everything by means of cunning and deception, lies and cynicism. It was generally accepted that there were many who made use of ecclesiastical privileges for their own ends, without any intention of taking their duties seriously.

Art is the best of all criterions indicating how deeply a philosophy of life or a class of people is rooted in a given society. The anonymity of the architects of the great cathedrals points to the fact that these artists acted as representatives of the faith of the people and were conscious of this, while the people recognized in their work a true expression of the faith held in common. The artists were sustained by the enthusiasm of the population, and the latter rejoiced to see their highest beliefs given visible form.

It can hardly be supposed that the records of abuses of authority and privilege which have come down to us contain more than a proportion of the cases which actually existed. If in the community of Christians in Corinth under the eyes of St. Paul himself numerous evils and abuses came to pass, how can we expect a better state of affairs within the world-wide Church of the Middle Ages, more especially as the position of ecclesiastical officials with all their privileges, authority and secular powers, gave them greater opportunities for indulging their egoistic desires and ambitions than were possible during the early days of Christianity. The entry of many unsuitable persons into the ranks of the clergy must without doubt have increased the possibilities of every sort of abuse. The faithful were well acquainted with the state of things; of this the numerous public comments of a mocking character are sufficient evidence. The classical example of Dante serves to clinch the matter and to demonstrate the eagerness with which earnest spirits desired a betterment of conditions among the clergy. Moreover, the numerous reform movements within the religious houses from the Cluny to the new foundations of the late Middle Ages afford proof both of the need for reforms and the fact of such reforms being earnestly furthered.

The period of the great religious conflicts marked the end of the Middle Ages, and the beginning of the New World saw the clergy placed in a different position. The conflicts did not remain confined to dogmatic discussions of an objective character; they were soon carried into the field of party strife. The personal element was brought into the conflict. Leaders on both sides were compelled to submit to an examination of their personal lives. The events of the past were dug up to serve as ammunition for one side or the other. Pamphleteers collected a large supply of material for use against the Church. The party standpoint often prevailed and both sides became sensitive to attacks of a personal character. As is well known, from the time of the Counter Reformation down to the nineteenth century there existed areas in which virtually the entire population belonged to one faith only: it is most difficult to follow the slow sociological alterations in the position of the clergy, for the tempo of these changes was not the same in each country and the effects varied very widely. As late as 1803 the old feudal order persisted in many of the German ecclesiastical principalities, while in France the position of the so-called higher clergy in the social hierarchy remained the same up to the Revolution, and in Italy certain areas were to be found under ecclesiastical rule even after the middle of the nineteenth century. Historical changes usually take place very gradually and imperceptibly. When they do occur the rapidity of the outward manifestation is made possible by a previous slow growth of underlying sentiments.

The peculiar phenomenon of anti-clericalism existing side-by-side with a complete devotion to the Church was often found, especially in the middle classes, in the lands where ecclesiastical rule was prolonged into the nineteenth century. In some Catholic lands in Europe this is the sole explanation of the religious position. Furthermore, it is well known that the so-called lower clergy at the time of the French Revolution were not always on the same side as the higher clergy. The education of the clergy, in spite of the Council of Trent, was not uniform. Contemporary movements, such as rationalism, echoed far and wide. In Catholic lands the field of higher education was entrusted to the clergy, who thus held one of the most important positions in the life of the people. The cleric always finds the best and quickest path to the performance of his special tasks, when he has himself absorbed the cultural treasures of his people. Up to the year 1800 humanistic education afforded the sole entry to all real culture; thus the position of theology within the educational field remained untouched.

The field of work of the priest up to the year 1800 underwent alterations that were slow and not extensive: the work in schools saw the most important changes and here new tasks were tackled in masterly style not only by the great pedagogues of the non-Catholic world but also by representatives of the Church.

The nineteenth century saw a complete change. In many lands the first ten years of the new century brought with them a revolution in the position of the Church. Still more important were the changes when the new political orientation was able, as the century advanced, to exert its full power. For example, freedom of conscience, freedom of the press, and freedom of religious belief and propaganda and a general loosening of bonds became possible when the machine age had prepared the ground. Their own proper task, the care of souls, was given back to the clergy while the bishops were liberated from many of their worldly burdens, but at the same time robbed of many possibilities which could have been useful in the care of souls. New tasks were created by the immense rapidity with which the religions mingled. A great stimulus was given to controversial theology and polemical sermons by this mingling and even more by the popularization of science. Much more significant was the fact that new tasks were imposed upon the clergy by the need for defending their flocks at a time when philosophical and more especially economic attacks threatened the Church on all sides. The mechanization of life and the loosening of moral and religious bonds created for a large part of humanity social conditions that were simply unbearable and cried aloud for remedy.

At this critical time revolutionary ideas spread far and wide, offering not only economic help but a new outlook on life, holding up to the masses the vision of an earthly paradise. The slavery of the machine age prepared a soil ideally suitable for the growth of such ideas, directed as they were not only against the state but against the Church, which was accused of being powerless to aid the suffering masses. The clergy were thus apt to find themselves acting as trustees for the socially disinherited classes and confronted with all sorts of tasks which were only indirectly connected with the care of souls. At the same time they acquired a position that exposed them to many dangers, and to attacks from a multiplicity of enemies. The priest tended to be drawn into the class struggle and thus hindered in his real work of saving souls, which must of necessity be carried out without regard to political conflicts. The spirit inherited from rationalism continued to be effective during the nineteenth century, influencing the educated classes as well as the working masses. The so-called bourgeois spirit was of this world and those who were infected by it looked upon membership of the Church as a species of insurance against the risks of death. The clergy acquired a strong influence over the working classes, but their position was weakened by the loosening of their ties with the educated sections of the nation.

An undue enlargement of the scope of the clerical office is always a dangerous thing. It is only too easy for the means to take the place of the goal or for the goal to be lowered to the position of a means. Many clergy experienced in their office a feeling of power rather than one of spiritual authority. In their over-valuation of earthly aims the true significance of their tasks was partly or even wholly forgotten.

One thing stands out above all others in the history of the clergy: the fact that their fundamental task has always been the same. Emphasis may have been placed now more in one direction, now more in another; such changes have certainly been visible during the long history of the Church. In the early days the position of the bishops and clergy was first and foremost that of liturgical officers. They were the guardians of the sacred mysteries. Their social and charitable activities were so closely linked with the mysteries that they were regarded as their effect and product; thus the priestly function did not suffer any change through these activities. After the time of Constantine the bishop acquired in addition to his previous functions the position of a man of great influence in worldly affairs, for example, St. Ambrose. This was further extended and strengthened during the Middle Ages also in relation to priests. At certain periods many, if not all, of the clergy were looked upon more in the light of executive officials than in that of guardians of the mysteries. It is a fact that now and then during the Middle Ages bishops were found to be incapable of fulfilling their liturgical functions towards their flocks, either because they had never been consecrated as priests or because their educational level was such that they were unable to perform the rites. However, we should not forget that such clerics rarely came into contact with the people; they remained in the background as compared with those who were occupied with the actual care of souls.

The concept of the shepherd of souls is not identical with that of the liturgist. For example, in the Eastern Church we find that the bishop or the priest in his capacity as liturgist is greatly revered although he does not practice the care of souls in our sense. It would, of course, be incorrect to assert that the care of souls is a modern idea, but it may be said that what we now understand by the term, namely, a watching over the flock to protect them from the perils with which they are continually threatened, can have existed only in the early days of the Church and in the modern period, bearing in mind that the difference between the two periods is easily perceived. Even today the priest is first and foremost the dispenser of the sacred mysteries, in other words, liturgist. From the standpoint of values this function must beyond all doubt take the first place even when other priestly tasks occupy most of his time.

The care of souls as practiced today has placed upon the shoulders of the priest such a multiplicity of duties that the concept of the priest as liturgist tends to sink into the background. Some of the tasks occupying the time of the clergy today could well be fulfilled with secular helpers. It is a remarkable characteristic of the nineteenth century that it witnessed a widening of the gulf between priest and layman, more especially in an emotional sense, although this was the very century when the standing of the liturgist diminished greatly in importance in the mind of the people. Needless to say, a gulf existed in earlier times; in the Middle Ages it was regarded as necessary, consciously realized, and given a specific social form, a state of things which, owing to the

Changes in the Position of the Clergy

privileges enjoyed by the clergy, often gave rise to sharp conflicts. But the gulf to which we refer is something very different: it is closely linked with the secular bourgeois spirit fathered by the French Revolution, although other spiritual influences may have played a part. The emergence of a new and different type of mental and spiritual attitude during the modern period created a new situation. The so-called "Ideas of 1789" spread more rapidly in France than in Germany and other lands, but the inner meaning of the ideas remained the same everywhere and the result was in all cases a progressive secularization of every branch of life. Life took on a purely earthly form not only in the sense that science sought to explain everything without reference to another world, but, what is even more significant, in the sense that it was lived without any reference to other-worldly values.

A variety of factors, economic as well as scientific, worked together to build up the general structure of the nineteenth century on these lines. Finally the most earthly of all, the economic, triumphed over all the others. "If the accumulation of wealth were the ultimate goal of life, the economist would be the king of society." Thus wrote Thomas Aquinas. Since this was precisely the position in the nineteenth century, it was inevitable that the economists should gradually acquire a dominant position. Together with this spirit we note an undreamed of expansion of the democratic idea, with a special emphasis upon the rights of the people and the derivation of power from the will of the people. Of course there are always rulers and ruled, and even when, as during the period of the republic in Rome, the rulers were changed annually, the fact remains that a few rule and many are ruled.

In such an age the Church found itself in a very peculiar position. Even among the multitudes of the faithful the Church was a thing apart, having nothing to do with the rest of life. It was like a Sunday among the days of the week. The Church should be left alone, but it also should not meddle in the affairs of life! It is a matter for the clergy who, although performing certain functions for the people, do not belong to the people. Is it not in reality a Church for priests? Do they not unite in themselves all the ecclesiastical functions? Is it not they who take the sole initiative when new ecclesiastical tasks crop up? Is not the education of the priest such as to make him a man apart? What voice does the laity possess in this Church? In a democratic state every citizen has the right to vote for the men whom he considers worthy to rule over him. But what right does the layman possess in the selection of bishops or priests? Is not everything in the hands of the clergy? It has even been established that there is no mention of the laity at all in the book of ecclesiastical law—known as *Codex Juris Canonici*—save in one ruling (Section 682). Ulrich Stutz, the well-known jurist, characterized this book of canon law as concerned solely with priests. At the very time when Stutz made this comment efforts were being made among the evangelical churches to realize a "people's church," and it was claimed that the church must fulfil again this purpose if it were to fit itself for survival. This caused surprise among Catholics since they believed that the doctrine of general priesthood held by Protestants made it impossible, at the very outset, for a gulf to form between clergy and people.

The term *layman* is derived from the Greek word for people, and it is understood in ecclesiastical circles that it refers to one who does not belong either to the clergy or to an order. The dispensation of sacraments is a privilege of the clergy, and the ecclesiastical authorities claim for the Church the sole right of the threefold office of doctrine, priesthood, and care of souls. There were periods when, for example, the population of the city of Rome, together with the clergy,

Changes in the Position of the Clergy 85

elected the Bishop of Rome—the Pope. No dogma stands in the way of this practice—only the will of the Church. The people in the sense of the laity have no legally recognized function in the government of the Church. Yet the Church does not consist solely of priests. The people or laity are not there on account of the priests; the priests are there on account of the people. How then is it possible that the idea should take root that a sharp division between priest and people, symbolized spatially by the separation of the choir and the aisle in a church, should make the Church the affair of the priests? In the Middle Ages this spatial separation was much sharper because a gallery frequently partitioned off the body of the Church from the section used by the clergy. Yet the modern notion of the Church as an affair of the priests was quite unknown. In the early Church the faithful, after a period of fasting and instruction, were "initiated" in a solemn liturgical ceremony to the sacred mysteries. It is easy to see that the consciousness of belonging to the Christian community must have been of a very different order from that which is probable in the case of modern members.

The modern outlook is derived from a variety of causes. In the first place we have to consider the change in the meaning attached to the word *people*. The sense in which the term *Church-people* is now used is a departure from the meaning attached to "people" as ordinarily employed. The Church and the Christian community should constitute a unity, a self-contained organic body, in which all the members depend upon each other as in the human body. The basis of this unity is not of an earthly nature; it is not language or blood; it is spiritual and invisible. Today the concept "people" has acquired a powerful significance; it is therefore most important that when the term is used in an analogous sense (as in "church-people") that we should be clear in our minds as to its precise meaning!

The unity of a people is natural and direct. It is rooted in a basic reality however much individual members of a given people may seek to destroy or deny it. It may naturally be recognized, affirmed and given a deeper meaning in the mental and spiritual world. "People" signifies something more than a group of human beings related by blood; its greatest strength is demonstrated in the field of cultural value and most of all in the language. On the other hand the unity of the Church must first be affirmed through the acceptance of the divine gift of grace, as signified in the call to enter the Church. It is therefore objectively given in the mystical body of Christ and reaches far beyond the limitations of the term "people." But this unity rests upon belief; it is not present in an empirical sense, despite the visible unity of the Church. It is an object of faith as the confession of faith demonstrates; and as such it surpasses by far all that can possibly be understood by earthly unity and community. On the other hand this unity strives towards visible manifestation, since the Church is composed of human beings, who are formed of flesh as well as spirit. Thus, the Church as a whole and each separate community are witnesses of this visible unity.

In making use of the term "people" in the popular sense it is important to remember that ever since the days of the French Revolution the word "people" claims to signify not only the object of government but also the subject; not only does the government concern itself with the people as the object of its activities but the will of the people determines who rules and how he rules. The rulers feel themselves to be no more than the representatives of a community united in blood and by cultural ties. Seen from without the "people" form a great cultural and political unity; seen from within they are also recognizable as a great unity, although not all, but only a few, of its members can be concerned with the actual task of government. The position of the Church, however, regarded as a unity, is quite different from that of a "people." Still less can the sovereignty of the Church be derived from any sort of popular will. The Church is the bearer of revelation, the guardian of the *depositum fidei;* it brings the Message, the Word of God, to the people. The bishops, as Christ's deputies, have the power to teach; the laity have the obligation to hear that teaching. The authority is derived from the command of the Son of God and is not in any way dependent upon the will of the "people." The power to consecrate priests and to control Church affairs by which the Church is renewed and maintained is of the same derivation. The power and authority of the leaders of the Church is not based upon any earthly realm. It therefore makes no difference if at one time the people played a part in the election of bishops, or at another, secular rulers such as kings or princes, or whether such appointment was determined solely by the hierarchy. In any case the actual authority by which the bishop was empowered to proclaim the Gospel, to govern his flock, and to consecrate priests is not derived from an earthly source, but alone from the command of Christ. This is the belief of the Church.

The democratization of the modern mentality and the general acceptance of the principle of the sovereignty of the people causes the type of authority described above to stand out as peculiar, if not incomprehensible. From the standpoint of the outsider it would appear that the ruling section renews itself, even if this occurs in a democratic fashion—since it is a matter of principle that every suitable member can rise to any place in the hierarchy—while the body of members subject to the rulers are permitted to hear the preaching of the word and to receive the sacraments without having even the smallest influence upon events. Views of a social and political character radiate their influence in every direction so that a certain tension within the Church itself could hardly fail to arise from the spread of the democratizing process. More dangerous than this development, however, is that secularization of the spirit of which we have spoken. The modern man does not feel the sacred truths of his faith to be so much a part of his life as they were for the man of an earlier time when the whole of society was formed and permeated by these truths. His knowledge of the Church and its values is not a vital possession filling him with joy; it is rather a piece of acquired knowledge more or less unwillingly assimilated through instruction. At certain times the sermon or the liturgy may touch him, but he brings no personal contribution to either, or so he feels. His whole heart and soul is not in the Church. Has a layman any rights at all in the Church?, he is inclined to ask. As far as doctrine is concerned he has nothing to do but listen. The constitutional aspects of the Church are the concern of the clergy, and the liturgy is determined by the Church and is quite outside the field of influence of the people.

Yet who will deny that the people are as necessary for the Church as the clergy? Not only are they necessary as an object of the teaching and care of the Church, but far more as an integral portion of the coming Kingdom of God. The concepts government, governors, and governed can be applied to the Church only in an analogous sense. There is in the Church no government in the secular sense. Though the pope, the bishops, and priests are the official representatives of Christ, each baptized person is a member of Christ's mystical body. The different members of this body do not all have the same tasks, but fundamentally the Christian is united through baptism with the priesthood of Christ. He acquires the right, when necessary, to confer the sacrament of baptism and through confirmation is declared specifically to be of age. He has rights in the Church as well as duties, for the duties of the bishops and clergy constitute the rights of the laity.

The development of doctrine and of the liturgy is by no means dependent solely upon the so-called government of the Church. It is perfectly clear that in the early days of the Church the whole body of members took part in the progressive life of the Church. Though it would be difficult to define exactly how much influence the people have upon liturgical development, it cannot be doubted that such influence exists. There are customs coming from the people which have, by the sanction of the Church, been incorporated into the liturgy. This kind of liturgical development is less visible today than formerly. This is due to the general development of the Church as a whole. Changes in the liturgy are at once apparent when really new matter, derived from the people, is incorporated in the Church. There is also a piety of the people which is tolerated and protected by the Church; this piety is partly derived from the liturgical life itself and is partly a parallel development enveloping the formal element after the fashion in which custom surrounds moral values. In the liturgy itself the layman is by no means limited to a passive participation. The oldest form of prayer, the litany, consisted in invocations and replies from the congregation: the liturgy envisages cooperation between the liturgist and all who stand with him around the altar. During the last few decades many statements issued by the popes have made it clear that the Church earnestly desires the cooperation of the laity in the care of souls. This may be described as a lay apostolate or by some other name; what is important is that the Church has always wished to see every member of its body lending aid in furthering the Kingdom of God. It is by no means out of the question that laymen should be entrusted by bishops with the active spreading of the Word. In former times laymen cooperated in the work of theology and it is not clear why they should be excluded from this form of apostolate. Still less should there be any objection to lay help in the charitable activities of the Church and in keeping a watchful eye upon doubtful cases and those in danger of backsliding. It may be true that here the help of educated men is of the most value, but this fact should not lead us to the view that priests and laymen should be kept apart; on the contrary, it should make us advocates of an organic and hierarchically ordered unity and the cooperation of the forces of the Church.

It is the concept of the mystical body of Christ with all its depth of meaning that can lead us to the true and original valuation of priestly functions and to the right relationship between priest and people. It will then be seen that the office of dispenser of the sacred mysteries, and the service of the Word take the first place. All the other tasks are derived from these. This first and most important task is fulfilled by the priest only as the representative of Christ: this, and not the personality of the priest, is the decisive factor. The indissoluble unity of the community of the faithful, an organic living whole as we see from the Scriptures, is rooted in Christ Himself. In this whole each has his own task according to his calling; the layman as well as the priest. The Church is not only the affair of the clergy; it is the affair of all the faithful.

ChAPTER 8 · Criticism of the Church in Modern Times

IT IS often said that no criticism is possible within the Church. This is perhaps one of the most frequently expressed grounds of attack. This charge must be seriously examined; we must ask on what grounds it rests and what is in actual fact the position of the Church.

We must ask: who is the subject of this criticism and who is the object; who takes offense and what is the basis of such offense? In the first place there are Catholics living within the Church who are affected by its regulations and have to follow them. These regulations may come from the highest authority, from the pope and the bishops; or they may originate from those in a close relationship to the members, from a particular priest or spiritual director. To the Catholic it is forbidden to criticize the substance of his faith, the dogmas definitely laid down. This may be difficult to understand for those outside the Church, but for the faithful it is self-evident. The life of faith may be disturbed by attacks from outside; doubts may arise and, with these doubts, criticism. But this is not the normal case. More often the difficulties develop at those points where the Church comes into direct contact with the world and its affairs. Criticism is apt to begin when the pope or the bishops in their official position take up a certain attitude towards some problem that only indirectly concerns the life of faith and morals, when the bishops, as they are bound to do, formulate some demand addressed to the faithful, or when the pope takes particular steps with regard to the position of the Church in this or that country. We can all recollect many occasions during the last few decades when the Church was exposed to sharp and even extravagant criticism. One need only think of the struggle that raged around Modernism. The violent excitement that moved large circles outside the Church invaded the Church itself, and in the ranks of the believers one heard not a few critical remarks directed against the Encyclical [*Pascendi*] and the demands made upon ecclesiastics and scholars within the Church. Every branch of ecclesiastical life was at one time or another affected by this critical wave. The attack was often directed against some point where the critics thought the Church should take action or speak out, when as a matter of fact it did not. Or the critics objected to the Church's forbidding something which in their view had a proper place within the Church. A third line of attack consisted in denouncing the failure of the Church to pursue what the critics regarded as a progressive policy with sufficient speed and energy.

It is advisable to make a clear-cut division between the type of criticism that comes wholly from outside, and that which springs from within the Church. The significance of the first is that it indicates to those within the Church the nature of the chief stumbling blocks for those outside. It is also possible that a non-Catholic should criticize the Church and its policies in an open and honest fashion without rancor, explaining, according to his deepest conviction, what is wrong with the Church. This sort of criticism is not so common; for those who could practice it do not usually express themselves publicly. But even an embittered and hostile criticism from outside is not without importance, since Christians should live in a spirit of self-recollection and inward examination. Christ uttered a clear call to repentance. This was not directed solely to those whom He addressed: it is valid for the Church in all ages, and for the whole body of Christians as well as for each individual. If a sore spot be pointed out in the Church, this may be done so that the wound is not only indicated but thereby made more painful. The individual Christian and the Church can learn even from such criticism: they should not ignore anything that is justified.

A more important point is the question: is it permissible for the faithful to practice justifiable public criticism directed against the arrangements or directives of their leaders and pastors? At this point a number of important distinctions should be made. In the first place do not let us forget that we live in an age of freedom of the press and of a wild chaos in the expression of opinion. It was regarded as a leading achievement of rationalism that everybody should be entitled not only to their own religious opinions but to the right to carry on propaganda. A special sign of freedom was the right of every citizen, even of the lowest grade of education, to practice unrestricted criticism of the opinions of others.

Thus, since the period of rationalism and more especially since the rise of the press to a position of such immense influence the Church has been drawn into a zone exposed to cross-fire from all directions. In Europe everything done by the Church was made a public issue. But there was no corresponding growth in a real knowledge of the Church and its beliefs. To the average educated European of liberal opinion the Church remains a quite impossible and highly primitive affair. This vast confusion of voices was not and is not heard solely outside the Church; it penetrates to the ears of those within. This alone compelled the Church to adopt a defensive attitude and to "take sides"; it was unwilling to be driven into a purely negative position. Looking at this matter from the human standpoint, it is clear that those within the Church who wished to practice criticism found the ground cut from beneath them. The faithful now shared the fate of good patriots who will never submit to and still less support criticism of their country coming from a foreigner. They could not afford to lend any support to the attacks of outsiders, even when they felt themselves to have good grounds for criticism.

It will no doubt be said that Catholics cannot in any case air their critical views, since even justifiable criticism would not be permitted inside the Church. We may point out in reply that for more than a century the Church has stood in the open, exposed to every sort of attack: everything concerning its being and life has been from one quarter to another subject to rejection and criticism. History shows us that every type of criticism practiced by those inside the Church has immediately been picked up by outsiders and used as a lever to further their own ends. "Here is a weak spot in the front," they said, and they proceeded to exploit it! This has been demonstrated in every case—without a single exception. This in itself, practically speaking, is an answer to the question whether the Church can afford to permit criticism.

A careful study of history shows that an essentially different attitude toward those in authority on the part of members of the Church was prevalent in the Middle Ages than is prevalent today. In the Middle Ages a German poet was able to say publicly that he thought the pope was too young; and the greatest poet of all was not afraid to assign a place in Hell to the pope. In his journey through the lower regions Dante saw in a special circle the priests who had been guilty of receiving bribes: only their feet were visible quivering in the air above the holes in which they were plunged head downwards surrounded by flames. In the center he perceived—in his poetic vision—three popes: Nicolas the Third; Boniface the Eighth; and Clement the Fifth. A truly awesome spectacle! The poet allowed one of the popes to make a manly confession of his sins in order to prepare the way for a sermon delivered in prophetic tones. He said this dreadful punishment was just, because our Lord and Saviour did not demand money from Peter in handing him the Keys, saying only: "Follow me." The poet drew a picture of the terrible evils to the Church resulting from the conduct of those men called to be Shepherds of the Flock who devoted themselves to the pursuit of wealth and all that it could bring and not to the souls of those entrusted to them. We should look in vain for such an outspoken attack by a contemporary poet upon any representative of a worldly dynasty! The betrayal of high office, the desertion of holy duty, has never been so drastically and boldly branded as in these frightful visions springing from the highest level of human imagination: visions that might well seem too maliciously grotesque did they not result from the deep incorruptible earnestness of a great mind bent upon saving his Church.

We must not forget that Boniface the Eighth was alive when Dante wrote! We cannot doubt that his poem must have had a notable effect upon his contemporaries in the same way as a widely circulated pamphlet against a ruling prince of today written by the leading poet of the age would affect public opinion.

This striking case is sufficient to indicate very clearly that in the Middle Ages criticism of the persons and policies of popes was possible.

The usual vehicle for criticism was not naturally poetry but, as we should expect, speeches, sermons, essays, etc. We might learn much in this respect from the histories of the various universities or from those of the great monasteries.

The reason for this very different attitude in the Middle Ages lies in the fact that a single great philosophy of life dominated the entire field of human activity. We must envisage a whole community in complete agreement with the views lying behind its life and social structure. There were, even in that period, non-believers and doubters, just as there were princes of the Church who failed in their duty or even sinned against the Christian ideals. But such people could be criticized for the very reason that the moral and spiritual consciousness of the community could not be disturbed by such a critique. Christianity, the union of all peoples in their religion, the strengthening and propagation of the Faith, and the certainty that the whole of humanity was journeying towards an other-worldly goal, the fulfilment of the Kingdom of God: all these things were completely taken for granted throughout the whole community. Thus each individual felt that he would be injured in his deepest and most sacred interests by any abuse of authority or any acts of an immortal nature on the part of his rulers.

Very different was the picture after the Reformation and especially after the rationalist age. It is well-known that the numerous pamphleteers of the Reformation period occupied themselves very much with the morals of their opponents. The abuses in the monasteries, in so far as they really or supposedly existed, were the object of a most attentive interest on the part of all those who desired to see a speedy end to all such institutions. The development of printing made possible a much more rapid diffusion of literary attacks of all kinds. The Renaissance period saw a considerable output of writings of a dubious and often most offensive kind dealing more especially with the lives of monks and nuns. The monasteries and nunneries were not devoted exclusively to spiritual ends, to prayer and contemplation; they were centers of cultural and even of economic activity. Thus many were attracted whose aims were by no means altogether spiritual, and when we consider the custom of placing younger sons and unmarried daughters in such institutions, it is easy to see that, despite genuine religious feeling, many persons were to be found in religious houses whose vocations were more truly elsewhere. It is quite likely that the authors of this sort of literature had no actual intention of attacking or damaging the Church: perhaps they thought the Church could not be injured! But the following age, and especially the period of the Encyclopaedists, drew heavily upon these sources. Voltaire and his followers made a most pointed use of such material in their attempts to prove the incapacity or even the anti-religious character of the Church.

The same spirit bore evil fruits in the nineteenth century. At that time the Church was often not a living reality in the hearts of the faithful, a minority group in many lands. Superficially at least the Church seemed to be on the defense. Thus when criticism became vocal in the ranks of the faithful and when personal weaknesses in the representatives of the Church were exposed, a very deep impression was produced. It can hardly be said, however, that the reproaches brought against the Church by Voltaire and his adherents touched the real dangers and temptations of the Church. They were too far removed from the true values. The moral weaknesses of ecclesiastics in bygone ages played a larger part than scandals of the time as grounds for rejecting the Church as a whole. It would be absurd if the faults of an Alexander the Sixth should be laid at the door of a present-day Catholic. After all, would anyone think of rejecting the authority of the state because, in the past or in the present, rulers and princes abused their powers for egoistic ends? Such an attitude would be universally regarded as utterly foolish. There is in truth a difference between a bishop and a prince or statesman. The former preaches perfection and love and he should live up to this. But do not princes and rulers in general invariably maintain that they rule for the good of the people and have not most of them taken a solemn oath to do so? The faults of high ecclesiastics cannot be weighed in a balance against those of the rulers of this world; yet, if this were possible, it would be seen that the Church would not be the loser.

Yet, all the while the spirit of genuine criticism within the Church never died out. The condition of such criticism is the competence resulting from faith and the fact of belonging to the Christian community. The criticism of those outside, as we have said, should not be despised. But it is of primary importance that the faithful who have the life of the Church so near to their hearts should yearn with their whole souls for the steady growth in perfection of the Church. In this world the struggle towards perfection is always bound up with self-criticism.

We propose in the following chapters to demonstrate the living spirit of reform within the Church by reviewing a few characteristic observations upon Church matters made by prominent Catholics during the last century.

Chapter 9 · The Five Wounds of the Church

THE chief causes of offense that the nineteenth century discovered in the Church are derived from the spirit of the age, and more especially from the inheritance of the age of rationalism. This is easily seen when we examine the more outstanding literary documents of the critical spirit in the nineteenth century. They reflect the feeling and mood of an epoch, and, since in these days things move more rapidly than in previous centuries, many of the causes of offense already appear to us quite incomprehensible. If we remember this, the measure of truth found in the critique and the dependence of the causes of offense upon the age become clear.

No one will assert of Antonio Rosmini or Cardinal Manning, of whom we shall speak later, that they did not belong to the Church with heart and soul. It was all the more painful to them to become convinced that human inadequacy impaired the efficacy of the Church or marred the beauty of its face. Many criticisms of the Church had been published in earlier centuries: an examination of reform literature from the 14th century down to modern times gives a convincing demonstration of a burning desire for the perfection of the Church coming from within the Church. In this place it will suffice if we take a look at some of the critical studies lying nearest to our own age in time and in spirit.

The great upheavals in the Catholic world in the nineteenth century had their beginnings in the Latin countries. In this respect Italy played an outstanding role; a political movement towards national unity was in progress and the entire nation was in a state of ferment which could not fail to have repercussions within the Church itself. The leading spirits of Italy were concerned not only with politico-ecclesiastical events but also of necessity with the general position of the Church. It thus comes about that we have critical suggestions for necessary reforms in the Church emanating from two of the best known writers on Church politics in the ranks of the Unity Movement—Rosmini and Gioberti. The passionate Gioberti delivered violent attacks against the Church and its leaders, while Rosmini confined himself to exposing shortcomings in the Church and analyzing their origins, not with the view of injuring the Church, but in order to stimulate needful reforms.

Rosmini's book bears the significant title: *The Five Wounds of the Holy Church* (*Delle cinque piaghe della santa Chiesa*). He expressly repudiates any aggressive intentions towards the Holy See and explains that he has always found its mode of thought noble, dignified, and completely in line with truth and justice. His vision is more penetrating than that of Gioberti, who often did no more than repeat current politically inspired notions about the Church and did not even shrink from using the crude catchwords of agitators. Gioberti looked upon the worldly power of the pope as the chief evil and next the Inquisition and the Jesuits. To the man of today it sounds a little peculiar to hear that according to Gioberti the Roman clergy were following in the footsteps of the Greek and Russian clergy, and for this reason failed to keep pace with progress, lost touch with the age and with it the capacity for handling men and affairs!

The Five Wounds of the Church

But even in the case of Rosmini the grounds of offense he enumerates sound somewhat strange, although in some respects he was not unjustified.

The first of his "wounds" is the lack of cooperation in worship between clergy and people, a lack which he attributes to inadequate instruction of the people and the use of a dead language. The people attend solemn services, but their role is that of pillars which support the Church without understanding what is going on! A consequence of this state of affairs is the training of a priestly caste, a closed society with a language of its own and interests, laws and customs differing from those of the nation at large. It is certainly somewhat surprising that an Italian should write in this fashion, since in Italy more than elsewhere the popular character of the clergy is firmly rooted, sometimes in a manner that would hardly appeal to German tastes. The most important charge is that concerning the use of a dead language, the consequent formation of a priestly caste and the loss of contact between the people and their religious services. Since the rapid development of the liturgical movement in Italy, Belgium, France and Germany, it has been widely known in the Church and also among the laity that the language question is of primary importance for the Church, but that the chief difficulty does not consist in an ignorance of Latin on the part of most of the faithful, and their consequent inability to follow the service. If it were possible to make an exact investigation as to how far the services—and it is essentially the Mass that is in question—are understood by the people, the most surprising results would come to light. It would very likely be found that the people, speaking generally, are well able to follow the services, and that the so-called educated classes, who are assumed to know Latin, are ignorant to an almost incomprehensible degree of the essential elements of the Mass. It is not excessive conservatism that causes the Church to cling to Latin. On the contrary, the Church knows well that much higher values are here at stake than those attached to ancient custom. Perhaps it is because the Church so fully realizes the deep significance of language that it is so convinced of the necessity of holding to the traditional language of the ritual. It is not because it despises or fails to value the language of the people—quite the reverse; it wishes to see popular speech enriched by the liturgical language and the liturgy enriched by the language of the people. It has been shown again and again that it is entirely possible so to instruct the people in the liturgy that they not only follow the service as a whole but are also able to comprehend the full significance of the different parts. The Church is fully conscious that the faithful must be inwardly near to the liturgy and its forms, but it cannot permit the formation of a popular liturgy distinct from that of the Church and coexisting with the latter. Rosmini's idea that a priestly caste has arisen as a consequence of the language question is quite off the mark. His eye is too exclusively fixed upon the clergy whose energies are devoted to the celebration of Masses, whereas in reality the care of souls leads of necessity to a continuous contact with the people.

The second charge brought by Rosmini arises wholly from the situation then existing in Italy; it is concerned with the inadequate education of the clergy and the failure of the bishops to devote proper attention to the real task of the Church, owing to their preoccupation with worldly affairs. There is, also, too wide a gap between higher and lower clergy and this has lowered the standing of the clergy in the eyes of the people. The seminaries with their teaching staffs are not up to the proper standard, the books in use are of little value, and the method of teaching is wrong. A disordered condition exists, says Rosmini, all through the Italian educational system, for one section of the population receives a purely pagan education and another a specifically Christian; thus a deep division runs through the people. The remedy is that the bishops should again become the centers around which the spiritual, cultural and scientific life of the community gathers.

It must be admitted that there have, unfortunately, been times when the lack of education among the clergy has been a source of grave injury to the Church. But it is also true that the Church, more especially in the last century, has made the greatest efforts to provide for the clergy an education in every respect worthy of their high calling. It is certain that this education must be first and foremost philosophical and theological in character. We must not listen to those who would thrust theology into the background in favor of other branches of study, for such an attitude fails to recognize the real essence of priesthood. In every age there have been members of the clergy who were responsible for outstanding achievements in secular branches of knowledge, and the Church has rightly been proud of them. But, both within and without the Church, we find men who demand in the first place a literary education for the priest; they have no conception of the supernatural values attaching to faith and the care of souls and they expect aesthetic pleasure from a sermon rather than spiritual strengthening. The question of the training of the clergy will always remain important and difficult, for theology is not a thing apart from the age. It is bound up with the age and must seek to influence the men of that age. Hence, it must master the language of the age in order to preach the Gospel in this language. Every period has special concepts of its own, representing a certain type of mental and spiritual culture and these seem particularly important at the time. Every man and woman belonging to this period participates more or less in this culture, but it is dangerous when a man who is called to a spiritual task is able to participate in this type of life alone without really understanding it objectively or being in a position to criticize it. Theology must analyze and understand the spirit of the age, and the education of the clergy must not ignore this fact; yet we must not forget that for the priest theological education is more important than any other.

The heavy emphasis laid upon science and knowledge in general in the nineteenth century, together with the growth and differentiation of the various branches of learning gave rise to serious difficulties in the education of the priesthood; the concentration needed for theological training was endangered by the rapid widening of the field of knowledge. Although we must have specialists in theology, the priest must be something more than a man with a specialist education, even if his grounding remains fundamentally theological, since he must never cease to speak as a theologian when he is in the pulpit. There have come down to us from the age of rationalism quite laughable examples of sermons in which theology was utterly forgotten and replaced by the shallowest moralizing.

Rosmini's third point of criticism could suitably be met with silence at the present time. He charges the bishops in Italy with disunity and lack of cooperation with each other. In former times the bishops communicated with one another by letter and personal meetings and held frequent councils, and a strict system of central control held them together in their common task. Rosmini has in mind the bishops who are overwhelmed with worldly duties and have no time to meet together to consider matters pertaining to the welfare of the Church.

Even if this charge had a justification at one time, it is diffi-

The Five Wounds of the Church

cult to speak of guilt, because the occupants of bishoprics had grown up in a tradition which looked upon worldly power not only as an actual but as a necessary support of the office of bishop. This union of secular power and spiritual authority had the strong support of those sections of society which regarded it as a bond incapable of dissolution without injury to the Church.

The next cause of offense in Rosmini's view is worthy of special attention. It is concerned with the appointment of bishops. He complains that they owe their selection to the secular power, a method which contradicts the eternal rights of the Church and the established usage of the earlier days of the Church. Rosmini is convinced that the election of bishops by the people and the clergy is to be preferred to choice by the secular power. Here we see with special clarity that even men of distinction such as Rosmini were strongly under the influence of the change in the mental and spiritual attitude of society. In the Italy of that day the alteration of the constitution in a democratic sense was urged from every side. The one main hindrance was the Church, which became a stumbling block for all the liberals. Rosmini also saw the salvation of Italy in an increase of popular rights. What then of the Church?

The outward pomp and glory handed down from the Middle Ages which still surrounded the office of bishop was derived more from the worldly position of the holder as a prince than from his spiritual function. It is remarkable, yet easy to understand, that alterations in mood and attitude on the part of the state rapidly make their influence felt in the ecclesiastical field. It was thus inevitable that this conviction of Rosmini's provoked a sharp reaction in the Church. The nature of this reaction can be judged very clearly from the utterances of Augustin Theiner who said that "without intending it and very likely without in any degree realizing it, Rosmini would lead us to *popolopapismus* (the rule of the masses over the papacy), in contrast to *Caesaropapismus* (the rule of the Caesars over the papacy), so much complained of in its day; and the chains imposed by this popular tyranny would be most certainly heavier and more painful than those of the Caesarian tyranny, even in its worst and most degenerate times. . . . This new type of papacy would be the most brutal and barbarous slavery, a humiliation and debasement of the Church, leading to a dissolution of the last sacred bonds holding human society together." In the year 1896, Fr. X. Kraus added the comment: "Today we draw nearer to the evil dreaded by Theiner with appalling rapidity. We are confronted with the greatest danger which can threaten the organism of the Catholic Church in the face of the democratic transformation of society." Perhaps one may be permitted to point out that, as regards the appointment of bishops, the Church with all respect for tradition has always held in mind that the bishops to be appointed should not be alien to the people. But there is no such thing as a generally valid method whereby it can be guaranteed through some special mode of election that the man who is appointed bishop is perfectly fitted for his task.

The fifth of Rosmini's "wounds of the Church" is the abuse of ecclesiastical property. This is not used, as was the original intention, for charitable purposes. The process of historical development is perhaps more to blame than the individuals who were caught up in the process. Today many will find the enthusiasm with which emperors and kings endowed the Church with vast properties incomprehensible and unreasonable. What happened in reality, however, was that such properties were at once made use of for valuable religious and cultural purposes of real importance and value. Evidence of

The Five Wounds of the Church

this is to be seen in the great institutions of the Middle Ages which were in control of great wealth. When such great properties remained in the hands of the Church century after century, it is quite understandable that the trustees of this wealth should often lose sight of the original aims of the founders, yet at the same time look upon it as a sacred duty to maintain the property, more especially when it was possible to continue to further the cultural purposes for which the foundations were used. It may be said of the properties of many great families that they were originally intended for better aims than those pursued by the descendants of the founders of the family.

It is only human if those responsible for Church property should not accurately measure the proper function of the property in relation to the Church and, perhaps from a species of conscientiousness, devote their attention to an administration more suitable to a personal property. The trustees of Church property are human beings who feel responsible for the wealth entrusted to them. Who among them would feel himself strong enough or sufficiently justified to declare at any given time that the property was an obstacle to the true mission of the Church and must be given up?

Thus, in giving prominence to the "five wounds," Rosmini certainly made a characteristic contribution to criticism of the Church. He was, however, bound up with his time, even with the Italy of his time, and this sets limits to his criticisms and his positive suggestions. He sought to give greater effect to the mission of the Church and to free it from those human weaknesses which, if understandable, were nevertheless, in his view, to be fought against. He took care not to use too general terms or to make use of charges associated with the typical liberal spirit stemming from the French Revolution. The same may be said of other typical reform suggestions formulated inside the Church and placed before the general public.

We select now two characteristic examples: one from the nineteenth and one from the twentieth century. The first is from the time of the Catholic revival in England; the second from the early days of the twentieth century.

The former consists of the notes which Cardinal Manning, Archbishop of Westminster, made upon the position of the Church in England. Those outside the Church often suppose that bishops, as shepherds of the Church, do not expose to the public view human weaknesses within the Church. If a prince of the Church of the calibre and importance of Manning put down in writing his analysis of the reasons why the Church did not make more headway in England, that is the best possible proof that there are high dignitaries of the Church who earnestly seek to discover within the Church itself human weaknesses which cry for reform.

chapter 10 · Hindrances to the Spread of the Catholic Church in England

THE NOTES OF CARDINAL MANNING *were not intended for the public. All the greater is their value as a proof of a genuine critical will within the Church. The Cardinal's biographer, Edmund Sheridan Purcell, published these memoranda under the title: Hindrances to the Spread of the Catholic Church in England* (1890).

IT IS not necessary to examine these hindrances in detail, for the author specifically states that they are hindrances to the spread of the Church in England. There is also a certain amount of overlapping in the Cardinal's arrangement. The importance of his Notes is to be found in the fact that the author was not an ordinary critic: by virtue of his position, and even more by reason of his own past life he was the typical representative of a generation of English Catholics. To avoid receiving a false impression it is essential to realize these facts before reading the book. The matter consists of notes hastily jotted down in which the Cardinal sought to clarify his own mind with regard to the position of the Catholic Church in England.

History tells us that the Cardinal was a most energetic man with a firm conviction that the Church through his conversion had gained a valuable protagonist gifted with exceptional powers. As is well-known he came from the ranks of the Anglican clergy, described by Gioberti as a cleric cultured and urbane. In this Gioberti was doubtless right. Manning belonged to the more privileged section of this clergy. He was a product of all that was best in the English educational system. We should not forget that in making his decision to join the Catholics he threw in his lot with a body which, in his own words, was not as yet on a footing of equality in the eyes of the law and was despised or ignored by society. He came to the Catholic Church in England at a time when it had practically nothing to show in the way of independent achievement in culture, whose members, on the whole, were far from representing the better sections of the English nation. His contemporary, Cardinal Newman, who was a little older than he, has given an impressive description of the unimportance of the Church in England at that time. It was virtually debarred from public life; its existence was that of a sect, composed mainly of poor Irish people. It is not surprising that many Englishmen judged it according to what they saw around them. It is possible that Manning, the former Archdeacon of Chichester (1841–1850), allowed himself to hope that as a result of his zeal and energy the Church would make more rapid progress, and it is probable that during his period of active work for the Church he failed to understand many of its failures in England.

He begins by saying that the Catholic clergy in England were not fully educated, either academically or socially. But that was not a state of affairs for which the Catholics could be blamed. The greater part of the clergy in England were Irish, of whom Manning himself said: "Christianity is their civilization and before God it is the highest, but for this world it is not so." If this priesthood was not in a position to exert a deep influence in England, the reason could doubtless be found in the contrast between Irish and English. It is only human that even priests seldom rise above the prejudices of their people, and he found himself unable to bring any serious complaint against the Irish priests on the ground that they were reserved or even completely negative in their attitude towards English government methods. The tragedy of their people had penetrated too deeply into their souls for it to be possible for them to rise completely above it. Nevertheless, we must take his first charge seriously: namely, that the more a priest is bound up with the culture and tradition of his people, the more influence he is able to exert. The love of country which he demanded from the clergy is not forbidden to any of them; it is a demand rooted in the laws of God. The feeling of the Irish was for their own land and no one could be surprised that they could not feel in the same way about England. Every Catholic will be in agreement with Manning's declaration that an educated man should take note of all that bears upon the condition of the people and upon poverty and misery. This is even more the duty of a Christian and Catholic, and pre-eminently so of a priest or bishop.

This charge of the Cardinal's is not peculiar to English conditions. It could have been applied in the nineteenth and twentieth centuries to all the lands where political upheavals took place. It is enough to recall the case of Italy and the struggle for Italian unity. Divisions of a painful nature were created in the minds of those whose devotion to the Papal See was as great as their desire for a united nation; one could not expect from the majority of Catholics a completely cool and objective attitude towards a conflict which stirred up the deepest passions. Even the most highly educated men found it difficult to come to a decision in a conflict like this where theoretical considerations gave way to the interplay of fierce emotions.

Now, however, the political conditions have changed not only in Italy but in many other lands. The man of today no longer remembers that some hundred years ago the mingling of the different denominations was almost unknown: they came together for the most part only in the pages of theological journals. The passing away of the small provincial states of which, in Germany especially, there were so many, and their amalgamation into large political entities had the effect of bringing masses of Catholics and of Protestants together in the same state. But it has never been laid down that the clergy were forbidden to take up the cause of their people and country.

The second hindrance taken up by Manning was described in his own terms as, "shallowness in preaching." He has in mind, of course, the conditions in England, but we should like to pick out some points of general interest. He held the view that the basic beliefs of the Christian religion received too little attention in sermons and all sorts of truths and duties of a derivatory nature too much. In mission work, he adds, the preachers usually understood this, and laid weight on the fundamentals, but they were negligent when it came to the normal Sunday sermon. Above all, the sermon will not be effective unless it is reflected in the life of the preacher. It is a mark of the sincerity and genuine religious feeling of the Cardinal that he should lay so much weight on living the sermons and not merely preaching them, and that he should describe the inadequate preparation of sermons as the betrayal of a task given by God. The priest regarded from the human standpoint will be most affected by such attacks on the Church as touch him personally and by the obstacles which confront him in his own work; it is only human that a man will seek to follow the line of least resistance. And it may well happen that a preacher will select such themes as will, in his view, find

Hindrances to the Spread of the Church in England

approval among at least a portion of his hearers, or that he will prefer certain devotional practices not in themselves of primary importance. Nevertheless, the manifold differentiation that exists in religious life cannot be rejected and it would be just as mistaken for a preacher to dispense altogether with derivative truths as it would be were he to overlook the central truths and concentrate wholly upon matters of secondary importance.

The third point raised by the Cardinal refers to the widespread rejection of the use of the Bible. One may well, in this connection, recollect the words of St. Augustine, who denounced the neglect of the Gospel writings as one of the greatest evils in the life of the Church. In one of his sermons Augustine declared: "We praise God who gave us these sacred books. Let us not be blind when the light is shining!" (*Serm. 118*, n.2). A modern preacher, K. O. Rottmanner, O.S.B., says: "Do we pay attention to what St. Augustine said? Is it not true that, if the Bible were better known and valued among the children of light, a great deal of the superstition and ignorance, stupidity and faithlessness too often to be found among us would not exist. We, who desire to be looked upon as children of light, too often hold aloof from the sacred book which should be to us a source of truth and wisdom. If we took its teachings and precepts more to heart, if its words became part of our flesh and blood, we should not only gain a wealth of spiritual insight, but should find increased wisdom in human affairs. The lack of wisdom in the children of light is chiefly evidenced in their failure to place a high enough value upon human life and thought; yet this is also derived from God and stands under His protection and care. And nowhere more than in the Bible do we find a right and all-embracing valuation of this life; no other book gives us so deep and just a treatment of human affairs." There are special reasons for the popular neglect of this study in Germany and England and some other lands. But in recent years genuine movements for the study of the Bible have come into being in Germany and Italy.

The fourth hindrance is found by Manning to consist in the astonishing ignorance among Catholics born in the Faith of the moral and spiritual conditions obtaining among their own fellow countrymen. He reports many very strange opinions held by Catholics about Protestants and maintains that these opinions are so deeply rooted, especially among priests, that converts to the Church have in some cases been refused admission. Even when this was overcome there remained a series of erroneous views on the part of Catholics as to the religious life of the Anglicans: views which did not contribute to the effective life of the Church. According to Catholic teaching it is possible for those outside the Church to live in a state of grace, even if they have never been baptized, or, if they were baptized, to return to grace as a result of true repentance. His own experience as an Anglican had made the Cardinal acquainted with many souls who lived genuine lives of faith, so that he felt astonished at the wholly erroneous views held by many Catholics as to the religious lives of non-Catholics. He then points to some Catholic lands where a high percentage of the population live without the light of the Faith, yet where many great works of charity have been carried out independently of the Church. It is certainly our duty to examine this charge in its general significance, and if we do so we must admit that not a few distressingly false ideas exist among Catholics.

This is not solely a consequence of human weakness; it is more especially due to the spirit of religious controversy which so easily degenerates into the spirit of party conflict. A party must always be right in the face of attacks; it cannot carry on a discussion objectively for fear of loss of face. This is very far from corresponding with the spirit of the Gospel. The doctrine of the Church as the sole source of spiritual happiness, light and salvation, has so often been correctly expounded that every Catholic must know it. It is, however, a human weakness that, where there is a vital and fruitful conviction, those who hold it cannot understand why others do not share their belief and are apt to attribute disbelief to deliberate ill-will rather than to ignorance. How often have Catholic priests had to suffer the accusation that they do not believe what they teach? This charge springs from the same spiritual attitude as that found among Catholics when they are convinced that the refusal of non-Catholics to accept the teaching of the Church is due to ill-will. One has to admit a measure of truth in these lamentable facts: * there is probably no possibility of wholly banishing the spirit of party strife from the Church. Even the most embittered enemy of the Church may act in good faith. His life may even be more pleasing to God than that of a believer who accepts the Gospel, while living in an un-Christian manner. Did not Jesus Himself warn his hearers that, on the Last Day, the inhabitants of Tyre and Sidon would fare better than the chosen children of Israel? These stern words of our Saviour do not apply to His own time only; they have a special meaning for His followers in the Church. It is a scandal when the children of light turn their backs upon Divine Grace.

To the fifth hindrance Manning gives the name of "Sacramentalism." He maintains that too many priests dispense the sacraments in a mechanical fashion, while their lives do not justify their sacred office. The inner spiritual virtue of the

* In a letter dated 28th April, 1867, Cardinal Newman asserted that his opponents believed Protestantism and religious disbelief to be one and the same thing.

priest should correspond more closely with the office of dispenser of grace. It is undeniable that a species of professional danger exists for the man who is so familiar with holy things that he comes to regard them as a matter of course. There is, regrettably, no means of avoiding this danger. A charge often made against the Church from outside is that of a one-sided emphasis upon the *opus operatum*, the intrinsic efficacy of the sacrament, causing a disregard of the possible unworthiness of the dispenser and a general tendency towards an external piety. The true believer feels certain that the outward act is followed by the inner state of grace. We will not deny the fact that mere external piety exists, even though the teaching of the Church makes it more than clear that the sacrament cannot be efficacious unless the spirit of grace finds a fertile soil, that at the very least, the obstacles which might hinder grace must be removed. It can happen, without doubt, that believers may fall into the very human weakness of looking upon the sacramental act as a species of magic. But it can never be suggested that this weakness is bound up with the true essence of the sacrament itself. There are men and women who look upon the frequent reception of the sacraments as a routine, and there have been times when, for this reason, a relatively infrequent reception of this or that sacrament was suggested. One may recall the view taken in Port Royal, with its rigoristic practices, a view which certainly did not in general further the cause of the Christian life. But we are concerned with another question: is externalism necessarily inherent in the nature of the sacraments as practiced by the Church? That a practice repeated again and again tends to become customary, and in some cases a purely outward custom, is a fact deeply rooted in weak human nature.

The sixth hindrance of Cardinal Manning is "officialism." Under this heading he deals with the exaggerated confidence

Hindrances to the Spread of the Church in England 117

on the part of the clergy in the value and significance of their work in its official aspect, apart from their personal capacities.

"It is certain that, as the objective is overvalued, the subjective is undervalued. It is curious that in the Anglican body, High Churchmen are dry, and Low Churchmen exalt their own persons. In the Catholic Church all priests are High Churchmen. And there is a danger of official assumption. But for this we should not have had the hatred and contempt of sacerdotalism. I am sorry to say that even good priests sometimes swagger; they think to magnify their office, but they belittle themselves. . . . Unfortunately even good priests are not always refined, and they resent any hindrance in the way of their sacred office with want of self-control which gains nothing, and often loses everything. . . . I have often said that our priests are always booted and spurred like cavalry officers in time of war. But they will not fight worse for being chivalrous and courteous."

This complaint of the Cardinal could well be given a place in Chap. 12 of this book: "Occupational Dangers of the Clergy." However, the weakness so strongly criticized by Manning is not always the fault of the clergy; it is often a result of the attitude of the laity. Manning makes use of this opportunity to take up his stand against the order priests: he considers that they occupy too privileged a position, as compared with the priesthood founded by Christ. His reasons are doubtless grounded in the special conditions obtaining in England in his time and are hence not of special interest to us. That cooperation between the clergy working in the world and those belonging to the orders can give rise to a state of tension is well known. For example, in nineteenth century France a difference of a sociological kind existed between the two: it was customary for the sons of educated and well-to-do families, when they felt a call to the priesthood, to enter certain orders, whereas the every-day working priests came, for the most part, from lower sections of society. It followed that the schools attached to the orders were patronized by the children of the higher social classes. On the other hand, the secular clergy, who were separated by their special training in seminaries, lost contact with the more educated classes. Perhaps the worst consequence of this, in France, was that a lower value was attached to the pastoral care of souls as practiced by the secular clergy than to the more special care entrusted to the different orders. In such a case it is not so much a question of offense being given to outsiders or to the laity, as to members of the clergy themselves. The spirit of the great orders has, without doubt, played a commanding part in the history of the Church. Speaking broadly, the Benedictine Order shaped the early Middle Ages, while the spirit of the mendicant orders gave form to the ecclesiastical life of the Middle Ages at its height. The modern period brought with it new and more mobile types of orders which, in their turn, acquired guiding influence.

The priest attached to an order is apt to acquire, as a result of his position, a greater freedom of movement than is possible to one of the secular clergy. The field of work of the former can reach as far as his order reaches, or even further, while the secular priest is bound to his parish and diocese. In the popular view the activities of the ordinary parish priest are less valuable than those of the priest who belongs to an order. This is a mistaken attitude and one that is apt to give rise to friction, but it is very human.

Manning selects the spirit of controversy as the seventh of his obstacles. He finds fault with those who devote too much of their sermons to a defense of the Church against attacks from non-Catholics, in place of giving greater prominence to a positive presentation of Catholic doctrine. This charge, although made with reference to the conditions obtaining in a particular place at a given time, possesses interest outside these bounds. It is not the fault of the Church that so much energy must be expended in repelling attacks. The nineteenth century brought with it, as we have seen, not only a widespread mingling of Catholics and non-Catholics, but, at the same time, an unrestricted spread of erroneous and hostile ideas of every description. Newspapers and even more, the radio, have brought to the notice of even the simplest people notions of which they would otherwise have had no knowledge. The means of propaganda were available to everyone desiring to employ them. Hence the growth of polemical and apologetic literature during the nineteenth century. A sermon of an apologetic character may be at times simpler to preach than a dogmatic presentation, but, at the same time, it cannot be said that the apologetic work is superfluous. It means much more than a controversy with opponents, who will usually make no attempt to listen to what the Catholic says; it is directed, first and foremost to the faithful themselves and aims at a justification of the Faith to the mind and conscience. The type of apologetics which seeks to discredit the opponent's argument has not fulfilled its main object. If an objection is meant seriously, and is in itself worthy of serious attention, the apologist has the duty of answering it in a corresponding fashion. The goal is always the same: the strengthening of the Faith.

The eighth hindrance of the Cardinal is concerned with preaching. He finds, as we also, that sermons are too cut and dry, and often out of touch with the listeners. Bearing English conditions in mind, he held the view that the preachers should take pains to establish contact with ideas already present in the minds of non-Catholic listeners, and these ideas are not sufficiently well-known to the average preacher. He goes on to demand a greater simplicity and more self-sacrifice from priests and missionaries. The Cardinal refers to a gathering in the United States where, he says, the name of Christ was received with loud cheers, while hisses greeted a mention of the Church. This constitutes a death-sentence upon the human element in the Church, he continues, but a proof of the love and faith which goes out to Jesus Himself. As a cure for a state of things he describes as "frightful," he recommends genuine Christian love, *caritas*. But we must remember that true *caritas* cannot consist merely in belonging to an organization. Our duties to our neighbors cannot be fulfilled by the easy method of giving some money. The Gospel demands from each one of us personal effort and participation. The Church speaks of both physical and spiritual works of charity. It is a defect of the age that the two are separated, and in such a fashion that the physical works are handed over to organizations. The Gospel demands from us, as followers of Christ, an immediate personal relationship to the poor and suffering. It is not, of course, denied that organizations may be useful in an age such as ours, when organization is so widespread and so highly valued that it would hardly be possible to dispense with it. But that so many Christians believe that through an organization they can do all that is required of them is lamentable. That is doubtless what Manning intended to convey in his condemnation of charitable institutions.

The ninth hindrance is not actually raised by Manning himself; it is brought forward by his biographers, who tell us that he took note of it in reference to the Society of Jesus. The notes made by the Cardinal, in his diary, about religious, and the Jesuits more especially, indicate that he had suffered experiences that were disagreeable and painful to him as a former Anglican; he would seem to have generalized upon this basis. It is beyond doubt that he was unaffected by the anti-Jesuit hysteria of many modern circles. As a matter of fact, the Jesuits owe much of their unique standing to the fear that they inspire among those who do not know anything of them in reality, but are convinced that they represent something highly dangerous and secret. They would have cause to be grateful for these legends, were their consequences not so unfortunate. As the matter stands, however, one may well ask why the work of the Society is less efficacious than it was; why it does not go so deep or spread so wide as it once did?

In the history of the Church, a high degree of differentiation between the orders and congregations has always been regarded as a special sign of the efficacy of the evangelical spirit in the Church. The founding and growth of religious communities has always been closely connected with a high watermark, or with a low watermark, in the life of the Church. Great reforms originated within these communities and from their founders, reforms which spread over the whole face of the earth. As we should expect, the regular clergy had also their times of decline and decay. A crop of new orders arising from the midst of established orders has often been the sign of a need for reform. It is a striking fact that the old orders, despite the founding of new ones, have always awakened to new life, especially when they returned to their original principles. It is certain that the orders have produced their deepest effect upon life, when, true to their principles, they strove to be orders in the strict sense of the term. When the regular clergy become drawn into the whirlpool of modern life, the effect is often a levelling down the distinction between them and the secular clergy: activity and hard work are excellent things, but we do not think it can be denied that quiet and contemplation are at least as necessary to a right life. When the Middle Ages honored the *vita contemplativa* as the highest form of human activity, this was taken seriously at least as long as the orders which stood for this life practiced it earnestly. For a large part of the nineteenth century it was the fashion in many circles to look upon contemplation as a form of laziness, as an escape from work; such a life was "unproductive." Nevertheless, the world of today will again learn, perhaps too late, that restlessness and activity do not represent the highest developments in human life, and that activity in the community gains in fruitfulness in proportion as it is balanced, by sections of society deeply devoted to inwardness and contemplation. It may be true that the orders do not always make it clear to outsiders from what source they derive their significance and their power. But when this becomes clear, and men understand that real sources of power for a great community are to be found here, the importance of the religious life will again be understood.

[In many ways these last words of Father Simon have been realized, as the tremendous growth of contemplative orders in the Church during the past decade shows.]

chapter 11 · Obstacles of the Early Twentieth Century

THE beginning of the twentieth century marked a certain turning point in religious life. The idea, once accepted as fundamental, that religion was an affair of the private citizen was severely shaken and Schleiermacher's thesis that religion should be relegated to a purely subjective position was recognized on every hand as false.

This naturally caused men to look in the direction of the Church, a development which not only took place after the First World War, but was already marked at the turn of the new century. These beginnings were at first no more than indications of a new consciousness, but later, under the influence of the profound upheavals due to the collapse of European civilization, they grew rapidly. Men's souls again yearned after a true community and its significance. The need for symbols and a symbolic attitude again became a vital thing. That which men had become used to regarding as a mere ceremony was again understood as liturgy. The conviction that individualism was narrowing and inadequate grew more and more and the need for a change of front was realized. Many of the charges previously brought against the Church were suddenly seen to be quite unimportant; this attitude was due largely to a new realization of the necessity of the Church and to a fresh approach towards the true nature of the

Church. Many of the points at issue were proved to have been the product of conditions peculiar to special periods and many of the attacks against the Church were of a cultural rather than a religious character. In the course of time our standpoint has been corrected. Let us listen to some of the causes of complaint against the Church, as formulated by an Italian writer in 1906.

Antonio Fogazzaro wrote *The Saint* in 1905, under the influence of a particular politico-ecclesiastical situation. The book attracted great attention in Germany, where a translation speedily appeared. It was very soon placed upon the *Index of Forbidden Books.* Just as Cardinal Manning cannot be understood unless one remembers that he was an Englishman who lived at the time when Catholicism in England was beginning to renew itself, so Fogazzaro cannot be wholly understood unless one considers the conditions then obtaining in Italy. The Italian author deals, however, with the general cultural problems of the early twentieth century, and gives utterance to what many Catholics, in Germany as well as in Italy, quietly believed, without giving expression to their thoughts. In his complaints there is revealed an admiration for science which today is very far from being found among leading personalities in the world of science. Here again we see that time has caused an attack upon the Church to appear outmoded.

In his novel, Fogazzaro presents us with an imaginary picture of an interview between his hero, the "Saint," and the Pope, a venerable figure who is easily recognized as Pius the Tenth. The "Saint" believes that he has a special mission. This mission is to give the Pope his view of the state of the Church: the Church is ill, he explains; it is possessed by four evil spirits who wage war against the Holy Spirit. These are the spirits of falsehood, of lust for power, of avarice and of inertia. The

Obstacles of the Early Twentieth Century

Catholic Fogazzaro asserts, therefore, through the mouth of a fictitious character, that in the Church, as he knows it, there walk abroad spirits fighting directly against the Gospel teachings. He finds evidence of the spirit of falsehood in the attitude of many of the clergy and instructors towards science: these men call themselves believers, but do not realize how miserable and cowardly is their faith, and how far removed they are from the spirit of the apostles who proved all things. They are worshippers of the letter, who seek to feed grown men with the food of children; they fail to realize that, although God is infinite and unchangeable, man develops and acquires, from age to age, an ever deeper and more exalted conception of God and of His wisdom and works. Fogazzaro, describing this apostolic spirit, continues: men think that faith consists in accepting certain formulae; but faith is an all-embracing life. There is no need for anxiety in the face of scientific or intellectual progress, and no need to denounce as heretics scholars who fearlessly pursue truth, knowing that no truth can ever contradict or injure the true Faith.

Those who recollect the conflicts that raged in the early years of the century will find it easy to perceive what the novelist had in mind. This was the time of the encyclical *Pascendi* and the Modernist movement, a time now almost wholly forgotten. But we will nevertheless pick out from Fogazzaro's argument an underlying general truth: namely, that sermons and the care of souls as a whole should not be confined to a narrow intellectualism. The sense of inferiority which oppressed many Catholics during this period was grounded, essentially, in the immeasurably deep respect for science which filled the mentality of the man of the nineteenth century. It may be true that Catholic exegetical science was, in certain philological matters, not quite upon the same level as the corresponding liberal science; but one may regard it as a triumph for the conservative attitude of the Catholic scholars that, after the war, many evangelical scholars were loud in demanding that exegesis must become again a theological science. We do not suggest that it was Catholic scholarship which gave them the impetus to make this change, but it must be booked to the credit of the Catholics that they had never ceased to regard exegesis and theological research in general from this standpoint, even at the cost of neglecting some means of research necessary in themselves.

Perhaps Fogazzaro forgot, also, that in the Church the care of souls must take first place. Everything must be orientated in that direction; and for this reason it must, on occasion, be desirable on pedagogical grounds to withdraw ourselves somewhat from the clash of confused opinion, even if by so doing we leave an opening for critics to raise the cry of "inferiority."

Speaking of the second of the evil spirits, the author says that the clergy often fail to educate the people in inward prayer which can heal the soul as much as certain superstitious practices can ruin it. The reason for this lies in an immoderate love of power. There are many priests, Fogazzaro continues, who cannot endure that souls should communicate directly with God without an intermediary; they want to acquire power over these souls, producing thereby a weak, shy, and slavish state of mind. Thus the old Catholic freedom is destroyed. Obedience becomes the first virtue and subordination is expected even when it is not commanded; moreover, attempts are made to exercise religious authority outside the field of religion. The form in which Fogazzaro puts forward his complaint indicates that he has in mind particular political conditions in Italy. But he adds that his words are intended for the whole Catholic world, and that throughout the Catholic

Obstacles of the Early Twentieth Century

Church there should be a more intimate contact between bishops and people.

Here we draw near to the problem of the occupational dangers to which the clergy are subject. We shall discuss this presently. But it should be added at this point that the blame, if we can talk of blame, does not by any means lie wholly with the clergy, here accused of undue love of power. It is altogether too simple a procedure when the accused is charged with the sole blame for his faults. The Church is not alone responsible for a historical development that brought about a separation between clergy and laity and placed on the shoulders of the former one new task after another, including many that could just as well have been performed by laymen. This fact would not in itself have been so disastrous if, in consequence of the parallel development of the state, there had not arisen in the mind of the community a sharp separation between priests and laity, despite the intimate contacts between individual priests, often men of the people, and the general population.

The third of the evil spirits is described by Fogazzaro's hero as the spirit of avarice. There must, we believe, have been special circumstances, peculiar to the age, which caused him to make this charge, since it is hard to believe that the Italian clergy were conspicuous for worldly wealth. They lived, and still live, in a state of simplicity which might serve as a model for others. It is no doubt possible to be greedy for money without being rich. Though this applies to individuals, it can hardly be valid for a body like the Church. It is peculiar that the author makes a contrast between avarice, on the one hand, and poverty on the other, as if a poor man could not be greedy for money.

In spite of all this, the injunctions of the "Saint" are of great importance. He says: "We await the day when the preachers of Christ's Gospel will give the example of genuine poverty, when they will adopt the vow of poverty as they now adopt the vow of chastity, and when the words of Christ to the two and seventy will serve as an example." The Lord will crown the last among them with such honor as is not given, today, to the princes of the Church, in the hearts of the people. They will be only a few, but they will be the light of the world. History has shown us how great has been the importance for the Church of that voluntary poverty which it is here suggested should be extended to the clergy working in the world. This poverty was, in the Middle Ages, a matter of the actual conditions and not enforced by law. Today it is often, in the first place, legal, and the outsider may not be aware that it is also actual. The Catholic will realize that the individual monk has nothing that he can call his own, that, at the most, he is a trustee for things not belonging to him, for which he must render an account. But this is not what the modern world calls poverty. Even if few would change places with a monk, it nevertheless remains true that the monk who has taken the vow of poverty is usually certain that he will be free of material cares. He makes sacrifices, but, on the other hand, he gains security given to him by a community that supports and protects him. And security in earthly things is exactly what the world of today yearns for. Consider the host of insurances now possible against every sort of danger in the present or future. In many states, as we all know, men rely on the protection of the state itself when they cannot enjoy the benefits of insurance otherwise. Genuine poverty today would signify that an individual had surrendered such security from ideal motives. The kind of asceticism which consists in giving up luxurious or even good living is today, regrettably enough, the lot of millions who exist below a decent living standard and who are often glad when they can get enough to eat. To many of these the standard of living of many monks would very likely seem like wealth, at least with regard to the question of food.

Jakob Burckhardt pointed out, in the seventies of the last century, that a real improvement in the European position could be expected only from men of ascetic life. Today an ascetic would be a man who would give up the security desired above all things by the average citizen, making the sacrifice for Christ's sake and that of his fellows. But to belong to a great organization, such as one of the orders, represents a kind of security which is desired, though in a quite different form, by the man of our century. Because the life of today is centered wholly in this world, "security" is the characteristic symptom of the spiritual condition of the age. Throughout the centuries great orders sprang into being in answer to special problems born of the needs of the age. The Benedictines were the answer to the decadence of late Roman society, which was unable to stem the downfall of the empire, since each thought only of his private interests and none of saving the community. The mendicant orders were the response to the need created when the ecclesiastical organizations immersed in wealth and security had almost lost sight of their mission. The need for model lives, lived in poverty and insecurity, may be less obvious in an age when the classes are well balanced and there is a relative well-being throughout the community. But an age can come, perhaps it is already at hand, when the Church will hold a light up to its young people by means of ascetic men and women prepared to take upon themselves every sort of insecurity in the name of Christ and the Kingdom of God. It is possible that we are near to the time when the spirit of Christ will awaken men whose heroic acceptance of the need of the age will help to lighten the burden for others. But we must not make the mistake of thinking that new forms of the Christian ideal can ever be arguments against the value of the old orders with their rules.

The fourth evil spirit is described as the spirit of inertia: Catholics, both clergy and laity are, it is said, dominated by a spirit of rigid immovability. "They are fanatically attached to all that is past; they want to retain everything in the Church exactly as it was, even the archaic forms of papal speech, even the meaningless tradition which forbids a cardinal to go on foot, and would find it scandalous if he were to visit the poor. This is pure inertia, seeking to keep things that cannot be kept; it is a spirit that exposes us to the laughter of the unbelievers; it is blameworthy in the sight of God!"

These words were written by Fogazzaro in 1905 or 1906. It is good for us to recollect them, for they show us that things can change more rapidly than the boldest imagination could have conceived. Here we have an excellent example of what Cardinal Newman meant when he said that one of the greatest faults of critics inside the Church was that they could not wait. A strong resistance to change is always found in the case of religious tradition. The health and strength of a people are manifested in the tenacity with which it clings to its traditions; this applies to religious tradition also. But it certainly cannot be denied that a serious abuse of this aspect of tradition is possible. But can we not say of almost anything that is human, that it is open to abuse? It would be a mistake to assume that the Church has any interest in clinging to hollow and outmoded forms. On the contrary, it has shown in a truly broad and generous manner that it knows how to adapt itself to changes brought about by historical processes and to critical situations. In reality, what we are here faced with is a phenomenon going much deeper than would at first appear. It is highly peculiar that earlier ages did not take offense at tradition in the same fashion as do the men and women of today.

Obstacles of the Early Twentieth Century

We may well ask why, in the nineteenth century, tradition should so suddenly become outmoded and a cause of offense? Manners and customs are always vehicles of ideas and concepts handed down to us from the past. When these are associated with the Church we can always find a close connection with the essence of all that is ecclesiastical, namely, religion itself. It is readily understandable that men do not like to alter, still less to abandon, customs giving body to religious ideas, bringing them close to us and helping to preserve religious feelings in a truly human fashion. It is very easy to throw away the good seed together with the husks. Since the French Revolution we observe a growing tendency to turn away from everything connected with the outer aspects of religion: from ceremony, rite, and liturgy, etc. The bourgeois pattern of life which spread so rapidly during the nineteenth century, bringing urban conceptions of life to the entire population, gave strong support to this tendency. The French Revolution did not give us the brotherhood of man, but it put us all into conventional middle-class clothes. The machine age gave mankind an outward semblance of the ideals of 1789, then conceived of as being the inspiration of future ages. It is a remarkable fact that the theory of religion as purely a matter of feeling should so strikingly fit into the pattern. The expression of such feeling in outward forms was felt to be unsuited to this mode of life.

As we have seen, the sense of the importance of old traditions did not gain new strength until after the turn of the century. If a custom has a real content which can be represented in a reasonable fashion and, above all, corresponds actually to the true order of values, it cannot be wholly alien to any age. The rapidity with which every sort of ancient custom, outside the Church, faded away in the nineteenth century could not fail to have an influence upon popular feeling concerning customs with a religious significance. It is, however, a difficult matter to find the golden mean between a reverent retention of what is good in the past and genuine progress. The building of our great mediaeval cathedrals continued for centuries, and we can say that new styles of architecture gradually emerged; yet, in spite of such changes, these buildings present to our eyes a perfectly harmonious picture, in which the various styles blend together. This serves as a lesson to be applied to other fields of progress. Tradition must be preserved. It is the deep root, out of which true progress springs and grows. To cling to tradition is no mere sign of inertia or rigidity; it is often a sign of healthy life, more especially in the religious field.

chapter 12 · The Occupational Dangers of the Clergy

Is it permissible to speak and write about the occupational dangers of the clergy? This question must be answered by another: does anyone really imagine that the clerical vocation is free from special dangers? Did not Pope Pius the Eleventh speak of the dignity and loftiness of the priestly function with the very object of throwing light upon its dangers and the mistakes to be avoided? Every walk of life has its own peculiar sphere of duties, tasks, and difficulties, and its own distinctive honors and benefits on the one hand, and its special dangers and temptations on the other. Catholics are convinced that vocations, founded upon a sacrament, receive from God special gifts of grace to aid in the performance of duty and protect from danger. This conviction applies to marriage as well as to the priesthood. There are of course natural gifts and graces, special talents and capacities; these also are given by God.

In the eyes of non-Catholics and also, with certain limitations, in those of the faithful, the Church is represented by those with a religious vocation; we may therefore ask the question: who precisely are those who attain to this position? In the first place, all those who have felt this call and were chosen by a bishop, according to certain conditions, are human beings with all the consequences following upon this fact. They all belong to a people and each to a particular family. As an unchanging factor in life each brings special dispositions and faculties peculiar to his race and blood, with bodily, mental and moral qualities derived from parents and forefathers. Education can do a great deal, but it cannot alter these inherited traits, which underlie all that education has to work upon. A further limitation which every young man entering upon the priestly vocation brings with him is determined by the educational and cultural background of his people and his age. Dominating ideas and tendencies will affect him as they affect others.

We must ask: who exactly will seek to follow the vocation of priesthood? It would be absurd to suppose that only young men of an outstanding type feel this inclination. Just as there are various types of character and gifts, so there are many different types of men who feel called to the service of the Church. The only definite characteristic separating them from those who do not feel this call is the simple fact that they do feel it! We speak of this calling in the proper sense of the term, as it refers to those who have been called by God to serve at His altar; but this He does along quite natural lines by planting the inclination in certain of His creatures. For how should a bishop seek out his clergy unless those feeling a call place themselves in his hands? Certain objective qualities, rendering the individual suitable in the bishop's eyes, are of course essential. Together with intellectual qualities there must be, more especially, a character offering some guarantee that the candidate will be equal to the tasks and dangers of the vocation. An inclination towards the priesthood must always presuppose an attraction towards the religious life, with its forms and practices. The man feeling this attraction will have in his mind some concrete idea of the vocation, even if this be more or less imaginary and remote from actual life. The idea

The Occupational Dangers of the Clergy

formed by an outsider of any given profession is always liable to diverge from reality, for the latter can be known only through experience. The man who chooses what he regards as an ideal profession forms a mental image of an attractive kind, giving prominence to all that is ideal in his choice, without realizing what the hard reality may be like. This is human and unavoidable; shadows will not be present in the ideal picture. The young man entering upon a military career will dream enthusiastically of triumphant generals; the scholar will see himself addressing crowded lecture halls. Day by day work, with all its unavoidable worries and difficulties, plays little or no part in these fanciful conceptions. There were naturally times when to belong to the priestly calling signified sociologically something different from the present-day reality, times when the demands made upon the spirit of sacrifice were not so severe as in the more difficult periods of Church history. But the greater the difficulties the more the idealism of young people is apt to be stimulated.

It is inevitable that among those attracted to this high calling will be some whose enthusiasm is not genuine or whose spiritual life is abnormal. In the early stages, such types can hardly, if at all, be distinguished from those whose calling is entirely genuine. We live in a technical age which has torn men away from their natural conditions of life, separated them from wholesome mother earth, caused them to forget the rhythm of nature and to turn night into day. This age, despite its numerous victories over bodily disease, has brought with it a host of serious mental and spiritual disturbances, which may be witnessed in every section of the people. We have to reckon, accordingly, with an increase of psychic abnormality through the whole of society. The clergy can certainly not be taken as exceptions, since the demands made upon their mental and spiritual life are more than usually severe. No one can bring a charge against the clergy, because, at times, more or less abnormal members of the calling prove unequal to its dangers.

The variety of gifts and of characteristics to be met with among the general population will be reproduced in the ranks of the clergy. There will be those with exceptional abilities and others who regard serious studies as a necessary evil. But is there any so-called "academic" profession in which only men of outstanding abilities are to be found? We find priests who were born with the gift of easy and tactful relationship to their fellow men, and others who are completely lacking in this respect. Again, there are those with a happy disposition who face the difficulties and problems of life without feeling the burden, and others who are forced to struggle unceasingly against severe inhibitions and inward fears. The so-called "four temperaments" are to be met with in every combination among the clergy, as in the outside world. One man may be easygoing and weak, pliable, and prone to forgiveness; another stern, strict, and inconsiderate: both agree, however, in not infrequently regarding their natural dispositions as special virtues, a very human attitude. Some are inclined by nature towards generosity, others towards thrift or even avarice. Avarice may easily be taken for thrift and carelessness and disorder for signs of a generous disposition. Had Providence ordained differently, many a priest might have become a typical schoolmaster, or even a first sergeant. In all these differences there is nothing abnormal. Various temperaments and dispositions are given to priests, as to other men, as the underlying ground upon which they must develop their moral life and their cooperation with spiritual grace, and through overcoming the obstacles which confront him, as upon a field of battle, he can grow to perfection as a child of God.

One thing must be said with all possible emphasis: the

Church has always laid weight upon the condition that those entering the spiritual ranks must be healthy in mind and body. Not without good reason ecclesiastical law has laid down rules, not always comprehensible to the lay mind, in order to make it impossible for certain men to enter the priesthood. For example, a cripple cannot become a priest, nor without dispensation can an illegitimate child. Furthermore, the Church has always realized that intellectual ability, to some extent ascertainable through examinations and scholastic achievements, is of less importance than true strength of character, although the latter is much more difficult to test.

The candidate for the priesthood is a man like all other men, and therefore a man with faults. Instincts and passions are a part of the concept man, as much as reason or will. Catholic moral theology teaches expressly that human passions are not in themselves evil, that they are a part of the make-up of the healthy man. Even the animal instincts belong to the same category, for without these a man is not a whole man. The more clearly marked and the more harmoniously balanced are the forces which make up a man, the more complete and perfect is his personality. The widely held idea that the absence of human instincts and passions constitutes an advantage or a sign of superiority is completely erroneous. It is a lack of control and order in emotional and instinctive life that we can rightly regard as a weakness or fault. Catholic theology has always taught that moral perfection demands that we should do good, not only with our free will but also with the whole strength of our passion. Even a great scholar or thinker must be something more than a man of pure intellect; he must have imagination. The man who strives with vigor towards perfection cannot dispense with the foundation of a truly human, and therefore ordered, life of instinct and emotion. If we look among the great saints we shall discover many who made no secret of their strong human passions.

The modern age, and more particularly the nineteenth century, saw a widespread acceptance of an ideal of outward form by which everyone could be measured. Part of this form consisted in the denial, or at least concealment, of the existence of instinct and passion. This was a development of the rationalist era when virtue was regarded as synonymous with well-fed middle class respectability. To this everybody can conform without inward difficulty. Perfection was frowned upon as much as if it were a serious breach of the law. It is the tragedy of mankind that the most valuable qualities are, by virtue of what is almost a natural law, bound up with painful faults. We must agree, at least to some extent, with the French writer Joubert, when he says: "A man who shows no faults is either a complete simpleton or a hypocrite of whom we should beware. There are faults so intimately linked with the most beautiful qualities that we should do well not to rid ourselves of them!"

The more a man is endowed by God with gifts, the greater will be the dangers that beset him. As Deutinger said: "where great works are to be brought into being, sin stands in the background, marking down Peter as a man who could be found grievously lacking, tormenting Paul in manifold ways, and casting a lustful eye upon the great Saint Augustine." Everything that the priest, as man, brings to his calling must be placed by a special grace given to him at the service of the Kingdom of God. Grace knows nothing of standardized men; it knows only men as they really are and these men it seeks to make perfect in their calling as priests. Men chosen by this grace must be different, because those to whom God will send them are also different.

It would be a grievous error to believe that men who enter

the priesthood or an order become radically changed in their nature as a result of this step. Such an error must have disastrous consequences: in the first place for those who take over the duties of priesthood, and hardly in a less degree for the faithful laity who accept such an erroneous view. When a priest takes up the new duties laid upon him, he will be the same man that he was before, but with altogether new responsibilities. Does he understand the serious and difficult character of these responsibilities? This question can be answered with either "Yes" or "No." Because, however conscientiously and forcefully responsibilities and difficulties have been put before him as a candidate, their true range and depth cannot be experienced save through life itself. This truth applies to every difficult task in life. When it is a question of staking the whole man, regardless of risk, humanity counts upon the self-sacrificing idealism of youth, for the young are ready to take over the most difficult tasks with enthusiasm, without being able to envisage all their implications. This applies to big things as well as to small. We should do well to remember the human weakness, which causes many who have begun great tasks to choose the path of least resistance or to fail altogether at a later date. Even the heroes who went into the last war did not always prove heroic.

The tasks falling to the priest are clearly limited. The threefold office of priest, teacher, and shepherd handed over to the apostles by Christ Himself embraces the duties of the priest. Empowered by the bishop, the individual priest administers the sacraments, preaches the truths of the Faith, and acts as a shepherd of souls. There is a hierarchy in these offices. The administration of the sacred mysteries is the most important, while the other two derive from this first function. But all three lift the priest above the mass of believers, and more especially the celebration of the Holy Sacrifice, with all that goes with it, from the sacred place itself to the special garments: all these things cause the priest to occupy an exalted position and make him a part of the ceremony and the mystery. These adjuncts belong, however, to the mystery and are for its sake and not for the man who stands at the altar as a representative of Christ. The faithful know this. But it is only natural that they are apt to forget it and to transfer the glamor and the glory that surround the mystery to the liturgist himself, and to express this error in their attitude, so that the priest may, to some extent, feel that these adjuncts are related to himself. It is quite human that for a brief period it may be forgotten that all the liturgical ceremonies that center about the priest have nothing to do with him, but refer solely to the invisible Christ. If the faithful, in order more easily to overcome the difficulty of believing in the unseen, surround the person of the priest with a halo that is by no means appropriate, such an attitude, although understandable as a human weakness, is virtually a sin against the Faith itself. The ceremonies of the altar are sacred mysteries, making a claim upon the spiritual life of the Christian, and he cannot escape from this by putting a human being in the place of the divine. The priest is occupied from day to day with sacred things. The Church is well aware of the dangers inherent in this occupation; it well knows that daily habit can breed a casual attitude and sometimes one of mere mechanical routine. The higher authorities miss no opportunity of making candidates for the priesthood aware of these dangers. Nevertheless, the priest who stands before the altar of God would be something more than human if he did not often sink into a routine. The degree to which his inner strength can lift him above this danger is the measure of the genuineness of his original enthusiasm. But the demands made by the care of souls under present-day conditions are so trying that weak humanity too often gains a victory to the loss of the congregation.

The proclamation of the Gospel in sermons and through the catechism gives the priest a pre-eminent position as teacher of the people, one which rests upon the instruction of Christ and the Church. Keeping to this firm ground, he is entitled to resist all opposition or criticism, no matter whence it may come. But a priest, being human, may be tempted to go beyond the moral and religious truths laid down by the Church and embark upon his own opinions and matters lying outside this firm ground upon which he is not entitled to speak with the same authority. This danger is sometimes increased by an unwise attitude on the part of the laity.

If a preacher loses himself in matters that are perhaps important, yet not truly fundamental, this may be classed as another human failing. The field of activity of the priest consists, like that of other branches of life, of a multitude of separate and often very small tasks and experiences. The priest has to keep his eyes upon all these things. His theological training should enable him to keep in mind a system of values derived from the higher authorities of the Church. But, as with other teachers and indeed with men of all walks of life, he is likely to have personal predilections for this or that side of religious and devotional life. Much will depend upon the depth of his theological education, but he is liable to become immersed in secondary things or to favor certain forms of piety which do not find an echo with the majority of the flock. The age of plaster statues in our places of worship was an expression of a special form of religious devotion, to be overcome only when faith again takes possession of the *whole* man.

Finally, the priest acts as a shepherd of souls, guiding his flock with advice, warnings, praise and blame. The first of these creates a close relationship of confidence, and is practiced mainly in the confessional. We all know that difficulties in the field of conscience can be more oppressive to the spirit than any others; for this reason, a good shepherd of souls does immeasurably more good than the world knows or ever can know. Having gained the confidence of those guided and advised by him, the result will be a firm basis for all his work, one that can safely be described as unshakable. But human weakness steps in again: this basis of confidence is not always understood as it should be, either by the shepherd or by the flock. The man who is successful in the care of souls will inevitably find that his advice is sought out in matters that do not belong to the realm of conscience, and it will often be difficult for him to avoid responsibility. It is merely human if those who seek advice trespass beyond the limits within which the priest is, properly speaking, competent. It is, of course, impossible to say how often this has proved injurious to shepherd or flock. But we can be very sure that, in the course of time, this enlargement of priestly responsibility has much more often been an advantage to the flock than a disadvantage. This is especially the case in small remote country areas where the priest is often the only person able to give guidance, and to be the pillar of the community in all difficult times. It is easy to understand that the confidence placed by the community in their priest can lead to his being more or less forced into situations that have nothing to do with his proper functions, and it would be unjust to regard any mistakes he might make in such a situation as prejudicing the Gospel teachings which he represents. On the whole, however, the popular feeling that a man deeply committed to religious ideals will take his duties to the community seriously is likely to be correct. If there are exceptions, that is because priests are human beings not always strong enough to resist the temptations of power, even on a small scale, and open sometimes to those of a monetary nature.

In his calling the priest takes upon himself personal obligations looked upon by the Church as fundamental to his office.

A degree of religious devotion and activity is expected of him which exceeds that demanded from the general body of believers. The regulations upon these matters are made by the Church; they have developed throughout the centuries and have frequently been altered. It cannot be denied that a too outward and formal fulfilment of these requirements on the part of a priest is a real danger; another is that he may be less conscientious in the fulfilment of moral duties than he is in regard to the positive commands of the Church. There is without doubt a hierarchy of values in the fulfilment of duties. In the case of a priest, too, a failure to observe the commandment to love God and neighbor is the most serious fault.

A certain loneliness and detachment from worldly pleasures is required from the priest. Yet, among the clergy we may find as many men who need social life as we do among the laity. We may also find as many who prefer to remain apart from social life. Moreover, for all men, joy is as necessary as daily bread, and a life without joy is a danger not to be underestimated for the individual and for the community. This danger is even greater for the priest, since he cannot participate in all the pleasures of the community because of his position and his duties. In addition to these things we have in the Western Church a special loneliness imposed through celibacy.

The Church of the West lays very special weight upon the much despised and criticized celibacy of the clergy. Pope Pius the Eleventh, in his encyclical upon the priesthood, gave special attention to the extreme appropriateness of celibacy for those in religious life. But all down the centuries, the Church has pointed out again and again that the demand for celibacy of the clergy does not in any degree signify disrespect for the married state. It is well aware of the depth and power of the human sexual union. Nothing more important has ever been uttered on this matter than the few words of

Jesus Himself: "Have you not read that the Creator, from the beginning, made them male and female?" (Matt. 19:4). The Creator Himself willed this dualism of the race from the very beginning. Jesus described this will as an unalterable reality. "For this cause a man shall leave his father and mother, and cleave to his wife, and the two shall become one flesh" (Matt. 19:5). This natural law is therefore so powerful that a man dissolves the closest relationship and strongest tie in order to enter into marriage. For a man it is accordingly the natural thing, corresponding with the will of God, that he should follow the call of nature. Following upon the above words, Jesus spoke of continence as a form of life, and He, the Son of God, calls this form almost incomprehensible. But, for the sake of the kingdom of God, it is possible to choose this form. Fully conscious of the difficulty of such a pledge as that of chastity, the Church took up the standpoint that it cannot be imposed save for the sake of the Kingdom. It is important to lay stress upon this, because it signifies that the priest understands celibacy not as freedom from social duties, but as freedom for other and greater duties. In the course of the centuries the Church has made it clear that it yields to no one in the honor and praise given to the ideal of motherhood, and the Church knows well that, according to the law of nature, no representative of the sacrificial ideal stands higher than the mother. In wishing to see the priest free from the duties and responsibilities of family life the Church is justified, since the Kingdom of God demands the service of the whole personality of the priest. Naturally, there is a danger that the priest will not do justice to the high ideal inspiring his freedom, and be driven to adopt a form of life nearer to what is called "a bachelor existence."

We must not overlook other dangers leading to a breach of the observances undertaken by those bound to celibacy. It is understandable that these dangers will vary according to the individual character of the priest. There may also be periods when the Church is compelled to fight more sternly against those who do not take their responsibilities seriously. Often those who fail in this duty can be considered as indicting the time in which they live rather than celibacy, even if the time is one which waxes indignant about the clergy. Then there will always be people who demand the abolition of celibacy. When one considers modern literature, one might as well, judging by the casual manner in which adultery is accepted, demand the abolition of monogamy. The sum of good accomplished by the institution of celibacy cannot be measured by statistical methods. But we know that it is responsible for the initiation of great and outstanding works, and above all, for the important fact that the Catholic clergy remained bound up with the people. No matter what may have been his social background the priest in his parish was always there on behalf of every section of society. Furthermore, one must never forget that young men intending to enter the priesthood dedicate themselves voluntarily to a duty and responsibility the difficulty of which is specifically emphasized in the Gospel itself. This was pointed out clearly in the encyclical of Pope Pius the Eleventh. It may certainly be said that no one, at the age of twenty-five, knows himself well enough to be able to reckon with the difficulties of later life. The Church takes into account not only natural character and disposition but also supernatural aid, conferred through the special grace of the sacraments, and it is firmly convinced that a man, healthy in body and soul, who takes upon himself the task of celibacy, not lightly, but after a mature examination of all that is involved, may accept the task, relying upon the help of God. At the same time the Catholic Church is not without knowledge of a married clergy. Pius the Eleventh says in the above mentioned encyclical that recommendation of the celibacy of the clergy must not be taken to mean that any charge is brought or objection raised against the different customs legalized in the Eastern Church. This, in view of the very careful language of the encyclical, is an important statement. The Church has its own good reasons for clinging to the custom of the Western Church, and perhaps not the least of these is that it knows the legalized practice of the Eastern Church.

With regard to the attitude of public opinion towards faults of the clergy, a fundamental indication was given by Jesus Himself in a section of the Gospel of St. John (8:1–11). The Scribes and Pharisees brought a woman to Him who had been taken in the act of adultery, and they asked Him what was His attitude towards the punishment by stoning laid down in the law. At first no answer was returned; then He raised Himself up and said: "Let him who is without sin among you be the first to cast a stone at her." The Pharisees and Scribes stand here for public opinion. It was obvious that Jesus condemned adultery. Nowhere is the duty of faithfulness more highly valued than in the Gospels. For this reason, Jesus would not have opposed the recognized authorities in their judgment upon one sinning in this manner. In this case, however, when the judgment was given without competent authority, He took up the standpoint that only a person free of guilt is justified in pronouncing judgment. If we examine His words closely, we find He suggested only that the Scribes and Pharisees should produce at least one person wholly free of guilt, who should throw the first stone and the others could then follow. This demand gave them such a shock that they all departed in silence and left Him alone with the woman. The authorities appointed by God had the right to pass judgment upon an individual for his actions, and public opinion had the right to object to and condemn a certain act of transgression as such, but had to be cautious in passing judgment upon a person.

The Catholic priesthood seeks in the first place to be a priesthood; therefore the most dangerous sins and temptations are those which touch the core of the priestly ideal. A priest is not an official, although he has an office to which God has appointed him. Today, the term "official" has a secondary meaning, confining the task of the official to a specific and limited field in which he has to work in a conscientious and faithful manner; beyond this, the holder of the office has no duties. Official hours are the outward and visible sign of an official position. The duties of a priest are in not a few respects comparable to those of an official, but woe to the priest who looks upon himself as an official, available to the public in office hours only! Nothing is so dangerous to his office as stereotyped routine and secretarial work. His tasks can never be mastered unless the whole heart is brought into play and unless they are not regarded as the basis of his material life; priestly functions are not to be placed on the level of a "meal-ticket." This is not to say that order and regular work are superfluous. But the priestly task is wider and deeper and more filled with passion than that of any official or civil servant. Furthermore, in his case everything must be subservient to the Kingdom of God, including all work in cooperation with other clergy; as St. Paul said, one thing alone matters—that Jesus Christ should be preached! Unfortunately it is only human that diverse and perhaps clashing characters cannot work together harmoniously, and that thereby the care of souls may be grievously hampered.

But all these dangers, serious as they are, are completely overshadowed by the one outstanding danger, the inner loss of faith. It is very difficult to fathom the psychology of the priest who, unknown to the world, lost his faith; seldom if ever has an adequate description or analysis been given of such a state of mind. The death of the life of faith is the greatest of all dangers not only for the priest but for his flock as well. This danger is even greater than the worship of success, described by Leopold Ziegler as, "the last, the rottenest, and the most shocking of all forms of human belief."

We have spoken of the occupational dangers of the clergy in order to make it clear to the laity to what temptations the priest, who is and remains a man, must be exposed. Christ and His Church have always desired that the servants of the Gospel should be men and should remain men. There is a profound saying in the Epistle to the Hebrews (2:17–18): "It was right that he should in all things be made like unto his brethren, that he might become a merciful and faithful high priest before God to expiate the sins of the people. For in that he himself has suffered and has been tempted, he is able to help those who are tempted." And we read: "For we have not a high priest who cannot have compassion on our infirmities . . . but one tried as we are in all things except sin" (*Ibid.* 4:15). These deeply significant words are further emphasized by the words: "And he, Son though he was, learned obedience from the things that he suffered" (*Ibid.* 5:8). When the Gospel speaks in this manner of the Son of God Himself, the pattern of all priesthood, it is clearly intended in the plan of salvation that those called to the priesthood should be and should remain truly human, even if they are specially distinguished by the grace of God, a gift which they cannot and must not attribute to themselves or their own merits. Not for a single moment must they forget that they are men like others; and it would be foolish to suggest, through any sort of pseudo-dignity intended to impress others, that they are remote from human nature. How can a priest help the souls entrusted to him along the path leading towards perfection, if

The Occupational Dangers of the Clergy

he is not travelling the same road himself and seeking to overcome his own failings and imperfections?

The greatest saints, and these more than others, have again and again admitted their imperfections. It is an open confession of weakness to deny, either by word or deed, the human inadequacy which is always with us and the moral imperfection which will not be overcome until the end of the road. Sacramental grace and priestly dignity are objective things. They take possession of the whole man, whatever his personal character may be, and use him in the service of others. The priest himself should find his happiness in the task to which he has been called. When the Church values this sacramental function above all else, it does not deny the humanity of the priest or fail to recognize the temptations and dangers besetting him. The fact that he remains in a condition of human weakness throws a still brighter light upon the grace given to the priesthood. When one follows the activities and achievements of the priesthood throughout the centuries, one is impelled to the conviction that no other institution in the West has produced results so beneficial, deep and lasting, in spite of all the mistakes and shortcomings of those who were not able to withstand the dangers to which they were exposed.

Priesthood and true humanity belong together. Jesus wanted His Church to be there for men and to be spread abroad by men. In his well-known paradoxical fashion, G. K. Chesterton truly hit the nail on the head when he said it was the beer-drinking, fighting, religious, sensual, and respectable man that we love and value. That which rests upon this broad human basis is eternal, while all that is built upon dreams of the superman passes away with the civilization that produced it. Christ selected for the cornerstone of His community neither the highly intelligent Paul, nor the mystic John, but one who was a quitter, a boaster, and a coward, in short a very *human* man! It was upon this rock that He built His Church and the gates of Hell shall not prevail against it. Other kingdoms have been built for the great by the great, and they have all passed away. But the historical Christian Church, recognizing human nature and building upon it, cannot be destroyed. The *weakest* link determines the strength of a chain!

We would not agree that the Church is eternal because of its humanity, for it is the life of Christ that bestows immortality upon it. Nevertheless Chesterton brilliantly illuminated this vital issue in his comments.

chapter 13 · Organism and Organization

From the beginning the Church has been a living organism set in the midst of the world. In its early days, through a process which can be regarded as quite natural, it arranged itself in small communities, and these were brought together to form a larger organism. The Church in its human aspect was a *visible* Church. But, in its essence, it was the City of God built of invisible stones namely, the souls of men.

The hierarchical structure of the Church belongs to its essential nature. As a visible organization, it cannot live without *order*. Yet order is a part of the natural world. Every kind of human society must live according to an order if it is to continue to exist. Even the most unimportant group or club must develop some sort of order. In the Church there is an immediate encounter of supernatural with natural elements. Priests and bishops are, in the belief of the Church, a part of the divine order. When a community has a leader, an order has already been created, in as far as the leader fulfils his task and gives orders. The type of order is determined by the nature of the community or group, the aims which it pursues, and the actions of the leader which will be suited to the nature of the group and its aims. The leader, naturally, is not free to follow his personal whims, to make his own laws. The line which he has to follow is fixed; in the case of the Church, the line to be followed is laid down firmly. As the Apostle said: "I have handed it on to you." It is rooted in the will of Christ, the Founder of the Church, and in the law of life which He handed down to it. But, since the community consists of individual men and women, and each community has its own individual character, the social and religious life of the community must become an expression of its natural life. The material with which a sculptor works, for example, has a character of its own which imparts something special to the sculptor's work, a gift which will not be the same for marble as for wood. The community, in similar fashion, has something of its own to say to God, the fashioner of its material. How much more expressive than marble or wood are human beings, since they have the power to make free decisions. God sets the design, but the human material makes its own contribution. The human element is thus essential to the fulfilment of order in the community. The message of salvation is of supernatural origin, but the mode in which this message is accepted and put into practice is subject to human forces, working in and through men and women. The individual never stands alone; he is always one of a community; thus an individual religious life forms part of the life of the community. The man chosen to lead the community cannot confine himself to proclaiming the Gospel. He is something more than the announcer of a fixed and unchangeable message. It is his function to take responsibility for ordering the life of the community so that it corresponds with the needs of the age and the needs of the men and women living in it. As a result, the community is dominated, not only by the order given and established by God, but beyond this, by an order that is a human development of this. Records of the early days of Christianity tell us that the apostles appointed a head in each community and gave him full powers by the laying on of hands: he celebrated the sacred mysteries with his community in the manner handed down to him. There is here astonishingly little in the way of order. We might perhaps call it the framework of an order. With this frame the man of today is content, because he fills it out with ideas and images derived from his own experience. It is a remarkable fact that both Catholics and Protestants, taking as a basis this scanty report about the original communities, are able to form pictures which fulfil their ideals. In reality, even in the early days, this was never more than a framework, filled in by the men and women of the time in their own individual ways. The goal of a Church community is supernatural: the union of men with God and the making of men blessed through the certainty of the goodness and grace of God. The community must become one in God: we mean by this an essential and truly vital unity, to be distinguished from a merely emotional unity, such as may be seen in love and friendship in the world. It would be possible, speaking theoretically, for a Christian community to exist composed of men and women unknown to each other, yet who could grow together into a perfect unity within the frame of the Christian mystery. In the case of family life, the blood-relationship, which is the source of unity, does not in itself create a perfect life; one feels inclined to say, unfortunately, that it does not, for the task imposed by the blood tie is so frequently not fulfilled. The unity given by nature must be understood and accepted by the members of the family; we do not, of course, refer to a purely intellectual understanding. The moral responsibilities in question must be fully accepted, together with the self-control that may be necessary. Yet this alone, as is well-known, will not constitute perfection, if the warmth of love and the emotional background, which to us is so vital a part of the family, is missing. It is the same thing with unity among the faithful. The fact that they are assembled together in a Church creates a visible unity. The fact that heads of communities and bishops, who are themselves closely linked, are able, by purely human means, to establish contacts, while at the same time confessing their faith and proclaiming the Gospel, results in the visible unity of the hierarchy. But, since the community consists of human beings, the basic unity creates forms which go beyond what is considered necessary as basic reality. The growth and development of the separate members, whose invisible head is Christ, is described again and again in the Gospels as an organic process.

In order to further this process men make use of means that are not an essential part of the organism of the Church and are, therefore, in the course of time, subject to various changes. The spread of the Church in the early centuries was doubtless brought about by means differing from those used today, and the growth of the Church in the Middle Ages took place through a missionary activity very different from that practiced in our time. The structure of the Church is, so to speak, fixed as to its ground plan on the lines laid down by Christ when He founded it. According to Catholic teaching the monarchical episcopacy and the hierarchical organization correspond with the plan established by Christ. Yet the position and functions of a bishop in the early days of the Church differed considerably from the practice of the Middle Ages, which in its turn was not that of today. But the structure of a community in the early days was not essentially other than is customary today. At the same time, we can be certain that the community of the early times was very different from a Catholic community in the twentieth century. The fact that a community consisted of newly converted men and women, meeting in the evenings at each others' houses for worship, keeping certain aspects of their religion (such as the Eucharist) absolutely secret and electing their head from the members of the flock, must have created an atmosphere and an appearance fundamentally different from what we know today, although the inner reality must remain the same.

It is always the case that the means employed for the preservation and development of the real religious life, at any particular time, acquire a special importance which we must not underestimate. Men are apt to attribute to such means a value and significance going beyond that which they actually possess. These means are essential to men, as human beings, because they cannot do without them. Feeling thus, men come to believe that these means are a vital part of religious life in the form in which they know them, and to regard a disturbance of these practices, which are in reality purely organized practices, as an attack upon the life of the Church. This brings us face to face with difficulties arising from the nature and form of the Church. The essence of the Church lies in its other-worldly goal. That essence, in short, is nothing less than union with the invisible, transfigured Christ. The means which according to the will of Christ always lead to this goal are few and simple, but human beings demand a variety of means, and create all kinds of new forms in order to arrive at the goal. Here begins the human element surrounding the inner core of religion, an element frequently having nothing to do with the sacred goal, save that it is placed at the service of religion. When these questions of form are given a value beyond that to which they are justly entitled, we have the entry of a falsifying factor into the development of the Church.

The modern age saw an immense development of science and technics. This was not confined to the scientific field, strictly speaking. It brought about developments in the art of organization, some of which were of use to the Church. The nineteenth century, which created the great cities of the modern world, produced, of necessity, new forms for the organization of life in these cities. The Church could hardly avoid taking over many of these forms. The brotherhoods of the Middle Ages represented a special form of organization adapted to the corporative ideas which guided the period and are seen in the social system and the guilds. The brotherhoods which corresponded in the religious field to the guilds fulfilled a very important ecclesiastical purpose, but later, by breaking away from the earliest and most important form of Church organization, the parish, they proved that every form of organization is capable of developing, from a means of building up the community, into an instrument of decentralization within the community. The early Christian community made use of Christian *caritas* to strengthen the life of the community, and permeate it with that spirit of love and goodwill, which creates even upon this earth an atmosphere that is truly and perceptibly Christian. In theory, as mentioned in the foregoing, there can be a unity of the community even when the members do not know each other; nevertheless, community life developed in such a fashion that the bringing together of the individuals composing it became important. A high value was attached to a knowledge of the needs of each one and to their alleviation. It was expected that the poor should participate in the good things placed upon the altar as sacrifices by the well-to-do members. The apostles tell us that the deacons were given the task of taking the poor under their protection and easing their difficulties.

The *caritas* of the early days grew into the numerous institutions for the alleviation of bodily and spiritual needs which characterized the Middle Ages. In the nineteenth century, however, the differentiation between the various branches of this work reached a stage which no one could have foreseen. There were communities which had to be basically rebuilt, and others which formed within themselves a world that did not belong to the Church. Not a few were formed in the midst of a directly hostile environment. On the other hand, communities which held to the old traditions grew to such an extent that the traditional framework was burst open. The early Christian body was a small but closely knit group, becoming more and more united in their religious worship. But the modern community is very often loosely connected, and it is necessary to reckon not only with enthusiastic and genuinely religious members but also with very many who are connected with the Church traditionally, but not in the deeper sense of possessing love and enthusiasm for the Faith. To bodily needs—a chief concern of the early communities—must be added the spiritual needs of those who are seeking for truth or who once believed, but are now shaken and doubtful, and, perhaps worst of all, the needs of all those who are scarcely aware of the fact that they do belong to the Church! Social evils which have arisen largely through the shifting of social levels and the contrast of wealth and poverty cannot be met, unless new methods in the care of souls are discovered. When it is no longer taken for granted that men and women belong to the Church, and when, as it is so often the case, "belonging" means no more than having been baptized or having retained a respect for tradition, we find ourselves faced with problems quite unknown in the Middle Ages. The power of social tradition is then seriously weakened, since an indifferent outlook is as socially acceptable as religious faith. This is not the place in which to discuss mission work, for the mission is directed primarily towards those who have never heard of Christianity. Nowadays, mission work often is presented to men who are uncivilized, or possess a totally different type of civilization, in the guise of a higher type of culture, rather than as a religious activity in the strict sense.

The Church of the nineteenth century has learned to differentiate and organize. More particularly, it has learned that it is difficult to preach to those who are hungry! It has also learned that it is immensely difficult to bring the Gospel to men and women who are convinced that, if it were not for a handful of wicked or stupid people, we should all be able to enjoy perfect happiness in this world. If it is so easy to enter into an earthly heaven, why should we not first make an attempt to open its doors, before we trouble to listen to the news of a hypothetical happiness, more especially since this demands all sorts of sacrifices?

It is not possible to take up the question of method and organization in detail. But we wish to point out that the Church is now faced with a dilemma that could not have been avoided. Is it not true that the Church was compelled to adopt modern methods in order to get into touch with the people? Certainly we have in the East the example before us of a Church that has always scorned these methods. But it is probable that this Church had to deal with a quite different mentality in the people. In the West inactivity has always stood for decay and the approach of death. Furthermore, the most harassed sections of the people are those who are most exposed to the propaganda of modern religious or semi-religious cults. The forms of *caritas* customary in the early days of the Church could not be sufficient for modern needs, just as a small celebration of the Christian mysteries in the house of an early Christian could not answer to the needs of a great city. In the old days each individual Christian was a missionary for the Faith. Today, few Christians feel that they have been sent into the world to act as missionaries. They seldom get beyond aiding the work of some organization. And, for the most part, the members of such organizations feel that they have done all that can be expected of them in the missionary field by giving a contribution. Usually they are convinced that there is no better way of helping the poor than by an efficient organization. That one is far from fulfilling the Gospel teachings in this way is a truth seldom present in the minds of the new generation. The work of organization was identified with the expression of personal feeling. In any case, whether the attitude of men and women in these respects was correct or not, the "outer works" of the citadel of the Church were carried so far forward that for those who stood outside and for many inside the Church itself was hardly visible behind its far-flung bulwarks. Since those defending the citadel were for the most part manning the outer works they seldom turned round to look at the spires of the Church far behind the lines. It is easy to understand that in this way the outlying positions came to be considered as ends in themselves and absorbed an immense amount of attention and hard work. A point was reached when it was not difficult to cut off portions of outer positions. But things to which a man devotes work, enthusiasm, and love, always seem valuable to him; often they appear so important to him that he feels he cannot exist without them!

The outer works of the Church were, of course, constructed through human strength and human intelligence. The architects had justifiable feelings of pride; they could set their work side by side with that of the purely secular world. An outsider might ask the question: what is the difference between a meeting of a Catholic club or group and a political meeting? The same economic or social subject might be under discussion in both places, but it would be dealt with from opposite angles. This need not detract from the reality of religious life any more than the fact that the Church in the Middle Ages, and later, gave instruction in Latin and Greek: humanistic education itself was an outpost of the Catholic system. That this activity was not a mission in the religious sense was fairly obvious, more so than in the case of, say, a social or economic lecture, given with a more or less apologetic background. Yet, in truth, neither Latin nor Greek nor any kind of meeting for discussion or social work is actually a part of the essential nature of the Church.

The only organization forming a part of the essential being of Christianity is the hierarchy and the flock, whether it operates very simply and with the scantiest means, as in the early years, or whether it has at its disposal a complicated apparatus, as in the Middle Ages and the modern period. Neither the mediaeval system, which may be called an organization of the state favoring the Church, nor the organization of the nineteenth century, which made use of modern methods, is perfect in itself and solely appropriate to the spirit of the Gospel. If both were to disappear, the Gospel itself would suffer no injury whatever.

It is undoubtedly true that modern methods of organization have produced an intensification of work unknown in earlier times. Even the care of souls has become a sort of work, at times even a bureaucratic or propagandistic work. It is judged and valued, as is always the case in this world, according to its outward success. It would occasionally seem that a most important Gospel reference to the success or otherwise of human work in the Kingdom of God is completely forgotten. Now all depends upon tireless, persistent work. The fact that the term "work" is applied to the care of souls is a sign of the times.

Along these lines, how can one avoid the thought that human effort is more important than the grace of God? It goes without saying that in the Kingdom of God everyone must perform his allotted task with his whole heart and soul. Yet it remains true that work, in the Kingdom of God, is a

Organism and Organization

totally different thing to secular work. Furthermore, modern organization rests largely upon certain bureaucratic forms, and these are fundamentally unsuited to the true nature of the Kingdom. It will be said that all these things are made use of with the object of pointing the way to essentials, that, behind all the outer manifestations, stands the salvation of souls. But the activities of men are dominated not only by the ultimate aims but also by the means taken to attain to the aims. In the case of spiritual things, wrong means are capable of so falsifying our lives that the innermost core of the personality is tainted. How far this has actually taken place is a question which must deeply concern those engaged in the work of organization. Has the emphasis laid upon certain values been shifted? This is a pertinent question, worthy of the most conscientious examination. In all activities of this sort, one must never lose sight of the fundamental fact that the work of the Kingdom of God was once performed without the aid of any of these forms of organization, and therefore, as a matter of principle, can be so performed!

If our courage and enthusiasm for the Kingdom of God rest solely upon our confidence in what can be accomplished in an outwardly visible form, then, when these outward achievements suffer a set-back, our confidence in the future of the Kingdom of God must be destroyed. That would be convincing proof that our whole work was based, not upon faith in God and Christ, but upon confidence in our own powers. Nothing in the Gospel teaching stands out more sharply than the fact that the apostle must suffer a defeat of his own self-confidence before he can become a genuine apostle. There are many characteristics of the modern care of souls calculated to give the impression that, in the first place, the self-confidence of the priest or spiritual director must be built up, that he must learn to trust more in his own strength, before he can lend effective aid to the work of the Kingdom of God. If this were really the case, it can signify nothing less than a falling away from the genuine life of Christianity. It would also lead to a dangerous position, in which the Church itself in its essence would come to depend upon missionary methods for the care of souls; in this way, the real progress of the Church would be seriously retarded. Our basic scale of values must reveal itself in our methods; it is a grievous fault when the organism is dominated by the organization. The latter should be no more than an instrument at the disposal of the living organism.

conclusion · *Civitas Dei*

SAINT AUGUSTINE, the greatest spirit of the ancient world, was troubled by difficulties similar to those now confronting the man of today. Augustine, who was a citizen of the old, decaying Empire, experienced the collapse of a great civilization. To him, this signified the passing away of a highly valued and familiar world. The man of today cannot imagine the deeply painful effect of the fall of Rome upon the Bishop of Hippo. When rumors began to spread, he wrote a letter expressing his indignation that it was impossible to obtain reliable news about the disaster (*An Italica:* ep. 99, Migne PL XXXIII, 365). It was his desire to share in the grief, to bear it along with others. In a letter to the Presbyter Victorian he says that tidings of disaster flow in from all over the Empire; news that specially grieved him was that of the plunderings carried out in Africa by Donatist fanatics (*An Victorianus:* ep. 11, Migne PL XXXIII, 422). It was not difficult to understand, said Augustine, that the newly Christian world should have been visited by such unexampled calamities. One must not forget that, although the Gospel spread very rapidly, it was also most shamefully despised and rejected. For his own part Augustine found comfort in natural wisdom: his biographer, Possidian, said that he comforted himself, again and again, with the saying *Non erit magnus magnum putans, quod cadunt ligna et lapides et moriuntur mortales* (the meaning of these words can be given thus: how can one regard it as something unheard of, that wood and stone should decay and fall and that mortals should actually prove mortal). How deeply he was affected is revealed also by his biographer, when he reports how the saint wept day and night. From every side, Augustine was bombarded with questions as to how it was possible to reconcile the disasters which had overtaken the Empire with the fact of Christianity. The pagans, full of mockery, were quick to point out that the Empire fell after it became Christianized, and abandoned the ancient gods; the Christians themselves asked anxiously: could their new faith not preserve them from utter downfall?

In this very difficult position, Augustine wrote the most thoughtful work of the latter days of the ancient world, *The City of God*, later to serve the young and forward-looking Germanic peoples as a foundation stone for their own political constructions. In this work, the saint places two ideas face to face: the *civitas Dei* and the *civitas terrena*. The question raised by the Christians was put forward in a simplified form: is Christianity, in spite of everything, merely a human affair, so that it can have no power to save the Empire? Augustine seeks to present the idea of the Church in its pure form. The Kingdom of God, he says, will prevail; its victory will be final and complete, but it cannot be shown in its perfection until the form enclosing the idea of this world has passed away. The *civitas terrena* is intended by Augustine to represent, not a direct worldly reality, but another idea, which emerges in human history as a force opposed to God. The two ideas fight with one another for the mastery of humanity. It is certainly tragic that the power thus opposed to God should still reveal itself in the world of the saved, and that men, in spite of Christ's victory won for them, have not finally overcome the world of sin during their earthly pilgrimage. For sin still exists among us, though all that is evil will be overcome in the course of history by the final victory of the divine powers, and not only overcome, but made a part of the great harmony, the *carmen saeculare*, the song of the world. The victory of the City of God is a certainty, but it cannot be anticipated.

The visible Church represents the *civitas Dei*, but in its concrete form, with its visible members, it is not identical with the Kingdom. The Kingdom of God strides through history, surrounded by storm and conflict through which the idea, carried forward by men and women, has to fight its way. The idea itself can *never* be defeated, even if the human beings carrying it go under, or if they themselves lose faith in the victory of the City of God. It is certain that the Kingdom of God in its idea and its glory does not depend upon human worthiness, power, or success; it will prevail in spite of every human weakness and unworthiness. Nay, the greater is the weakness the more glorious is the light of grace. Men should not be ashamed of weakness; rather should they boast of it! "I will glory in nothing save in my infirmities" (2 Cor. 12:5). That is definitely the Christian attitude for the victory of faith cannot and must not be the work of men.

It is not through the cleverness of men and women, through human inventions, mental powers or gifts of any kind, through human persuasiveness or wisdom, but alone through the power of Christ and the grace of God that the *civitas Dei* —the City of God—will gain the final victory, a victory that will not be made clear for all to see until the end. Therefore, we must never confuse human success, capacity, dignity or honor with the honor and glory of the City of God. The Church in this world has accordingly no cause whatever, not even the smallest, to deny or conceal the human qualities and weaknesses that are contained within it. However painful these may be, they serve to make plain the great truth that the Kingdom will not be founded by men, but by the Son of

God Himself, that its establishment does not lie within the scope of our human powers, but solely in the hands of the All High which will sustain it until the end of time.

There are times when it seems as if the Church must go under, submerged in a morass of human shortcomings and weaknesses. The wounds of the eternal Christ given to Him by men and often by the very men upon whom He conferred special favor distort the body of Christ just as once the suffering Christ was distorted. But terrible as this is, the day will come for the faithful when the mystical Christ, also, will speak the words that long ago were spoken to the doubting disciples by the risen Christ: "Did not the Christ have to suffer these things before entering into his glory?" (Luke 24:26).

A NOTE ON THE TYPE
IN WHICH THIS BOOK IS SET

This book is set in Janson, a Linotype face, created from the early punches of Anton Janson, who settled in Leipzig around 1670. This type is not an historic revival, but rather a letter of fine ancestry, remodelled and brought up to date to satisfy present day taste. It carries a feeling of being quite compact and sturdy. It has good color and displays a pleasing proportion of ascenders and descenders as compared to the height of the lower case letters. The book was composed and printed by The York Composition Company, Inc., of York, Pa., and bound by Moore and Company of Baltimore. The typography and design are by Howard N. King.

www.ingramcontent.com/pod-product-compliance
Lightning Source LLC
Chambersburg PA
CBHW050807160426
43192CB00010B/1668